HIGHLAND
JOURNEY

HIGHLAND JOURNEY

SADIE MURPHY

Matador
Unit E2 Airfield Business Park,
Harrison Road, Market Harborough,
Leicestershire. LE16 7UL
Tel: 0116 2792299
Email: books@troubador.co.uk
Web: www.troubador.co.uk/matador
Twitter: @matadorbooks

ISBN 978 1 8031 3526 7

British Library Cataloguing in Publication Data.
A catalogue record for this book is available from the British Library.

Printed and bound in Great Britain by 4edge Limited
Typeset in 11pt Minion Pro by Troubador Publishing Ltd, Leicester, UK

Matador is an imprint of Troubador Publishing Ltd

Highland Journey is essentially a true story, though all the people's names have been changed, including that of the author, who is called Sarah in the text. The cattle's names are their own.

ONE

NO MAN'S LAND

Once upon a time there was a beautiful field in "no-man's land." It lay between two cities and was surrounded by farmland. The only buildings nearby were a tiny museum, a small church, and two large houses. The field was not very wide but it was long. On one side a wooded area stretched down the whole length of the field. Along the opposite side of the field ran a narrow road. Close by there was a pond from which ducks soared high into the sky, spanning their wings over forest, field, and farmland. There had always been horses grazing, and they "owned" the field. They had tolerated the presence of two Yaks, as they had tolerated the presence of the two Jersey cows that had come to replace them.

The horses were quite prepared to tolerate the presence of two Scottish Highlanders that in turn had come to replace the Jersey cows on the very day this story begins.

The young bull, Dumpy, and the young cow, Rumpy, were horrified to find themselves in this field. They wanted to be back in their herd with their mothers. Having to share the field with three towering black giants made this new field a living hell. They had to get back home, or at least they had to try. Though numb with fear, that very night the two broke out of the field. It didn't matter that they didn't know where they were, or how they were going to get back to their mothers. All that mattered was to get away from the threatening field and run. And that's just what they did. They took to the cornfields, and as fast as their short stubby legs could carry them, they raced into the night. Their hearts pounding, their legs tired, they stopped for a rest. As they stood side by side, panting their fear into the moonlight, they heard the sound of cars in the distance. They concentrated on the sound of the cars screaming by. In the trailer they had heard the same sound right next to them. For hours they had shared the same road with these screaming machines. Could that be the road home? It had to be. Yes, now they remembered. It was soon after leaving this very same road that the trailer had stopped and spat them out at the feet of the towering black giants.

For the first time since their nightmare had begun they felt a glimmer of hope. It filled Dumpy with renewed energy. He no longer needed to rest. He needed to get home. In Rumpy hope released all the exhaustion she had fought to suppress all day. The separation from her herd, the trip in the trailer, the break-out – all had taken such a toll that Rumpy felt too worn-out to continue the journey. It would be more sensible for the two of them to rest until first light. Dumpy certainly didn't want to go on without her, so against his better judgment he lay down beside Rumpy and closed his eyes.

But he could not sleep. He listened to the sound of the cars on the road that would lead them home. Each car that screamed by seemed to be calling out, "Follow me, follow me, you'll find sweet sleep at the end of this road." Dumpy decided that he would scout the area and find the road. It couldn't be very far away. He would be back at Rumpy's side in no time. Rumpy heard Dumpy get up and move off, but within seconds she'd forgotten what she had heard and her dream pulled her deeper into sleep.

When Rumpy woke up, there was no sign of Dumpy. She was so overcome by fear, she was rooted to the spot. Where was he? What had happened? She gave a frantic call, but there was no reply. What could she do? She didn't know where he was, but he knew where she was, so she would have to stay put and wait. And wait she did. The waiting ended when Farmer Little found her. Rumpy was herded back to the black giants. The nightmare had her in its grip again. Her only wish now was to have her Dumpy back at her side. Where was he?

Farmer Little knew very well where Dumpy was, for early that morning the police had called him to say they had found his missing bull. Dumpy had landed up in a residential area. A young man had sighted him in front of his garage door. Having managed to herd Dumpy into his garage and lock him in, he phoned the police. Farmer Little sent his daughter Crystal to retrieve him. Farmer Little knew all this, but poor Rumpy didn't. She was numb with fear. Rumpy had been barricaded in her stable and it was there she heard the sound of the trailer coming along the narrow road towards the field. She feared they were going to take her somewhere else, somewhere she'd never get out of. Just as she thought that she would never see Dumpy again, now suddenly she heard Dumpy's call. She called back, not really believing what she had heard. Then the barricades were removed, Dumpy appeared and the barricades were immediately put back. Rumpy was overjoyed to have her Dumpy back at her side. Dumpy's joy was mixed with feelings of guilt. He had tried to find the road and failed. He had left Rumpy on her own. Rumpy licked his head and shoulders, and he began to feel the weight of sleep on his eyelids. He lay down in the straw, and Rumpy lay down beside him. Whatever else Farmer Little had planned for them, they did not care. They were together again, and they were worn out.

Closing their eyes to the nightmares that had been, they opened their souls to each other's comforting smell and fell into a deep sleep. As they slept Farmer Little and Crystal got to work fortifying the fencing around the field. It took them the rest of the day to get the work done. Though they felt assured that Rumpy and Dumpy would not get out again, they left the two barricaded in their stable until the next day. The horses quite understood the reasons for such imprisonment. The new arrivals had only themselves to blame.

Rumpy and Dumpy woke to the sound of the horses' hooves thundering over the field. "Oh to be running with the herd and kicking the air in play," they thought. But that thought was quickly followed by a memory of their experiences the night before. Dumpy hadn't found the road. Would they find it, if they tried again? And what about the cars? Dumpy had had a few near misses trying to avoid cars that had come glaring towards him in the night. They both wanted to be back with their herd. They wanted that more than anything, but the break-out had shaken their confidence about ever being able to find their way back. Dumpy had to admit that from what he had seen the night before, the field they shared with the horses formed an island that was at least free from danger. Rumpy and Dumpy decided to make the best of it and stay on the island. They really had no choice. At least they still had each other.

Released from their enclosure into the field again, Rumpy and Dumpy spent most of the day with their heads down nibbling on the short blades of grass. It was November and their field only offered small pickings. The horses ignored the new arrivals and kept well down at the bottom of the field where the pickings were better. Towards evening Farmer Little arrived. The horses immediately raced up to the top of the field and positioned themselves at the gate. It was feeding time. Once the horses had been fed, Rumpy and Dumpy were given their portion of pellets and a bale of hay and fresh straw was put down in their stable. A tub outside their stable was filled with water and then Farmer Little drove off.

With their tummies full, both the horses and the Highlanders returned to the field to nibble. In the evening, the horses stayed up at the top of the field, so Rumpy and Dumpy began to make their way down to the bottom. Suddenly, with hooves flying in the air the horses were upon them, biting at them as they chased them around the field. Rumpy and Dumpy ran like the wind and headed for their stable. One day they would have long, shiny horns to defend themselves with. Then those black giants would be running to their stable! But for now they had no defences. Their horns were short and they could only race like the wind over short distances. Time was on their side. They would be a match for those steeds one day.

Nibbling grass, being fed by Farmer Little, and being chased by the horses became their daily routine. Though Rumpy and Dumpy did not wish to be chased by the horses, the race for their stable was sometimes fun. They liked to run and, well, it was exciting; it was something different to do. They had their routine and so did the people in the nearby houses. Some took off in cars down the narrow road in the morning, returning the same way in the evening. Some marched past the field down the narrow road with their dogs in tow. That, too, was an early morning, early evening event. The dog marchers stared at the new arrivals for the first week but in time they walked past without even looking. Their dogs showed more interest in Rumpy and Dumpy, but luckily there was a fence between them and that suited Rumpy and Dumpy, who had enough trouble contending with the horses.

After a few weeks the feeding routine changed. Farmer Little did not come to do the feeding but sent his daughter, Crystal. Unlike her father, she not only put down fresh straw, she mixed straw in with their hay. They much preferred hay to straw, but when bored or hungry, straw was better than nothing. The tub which had always been filled with water was now removed.

Rumpy and Dumpy knew what that meant. When the horses had been down at the bottom of the field, Rumpy and Dumpy had nosed around in the horses' stable and had found the water fountain. Now that their tub had been removed, they would have to arrange their drinking habits around the horses' whereabouts. Crystal often stayed long after she had finished the feeding. She would produce brushes and groom Atropa, the queen of the giants. Then she would attach Atropa to a very long rope, and with an almost equally long whip she would make Atropa trot in circles, this way then that way. This procedure made Rumpy and Dumpy rather nervous. They felt equally nervous when Crystal took to riding Atropa at full gallop around the field. After such rides, Atropa would be covered in a blanket and served treats. Rumpy and Dumpy knew they must be treats, for Atropa gobbled them up and always wanted more. The other two giants, Speedy, the mare, and her son, Arine, the stallion also got treats. Rumpy and Dumpy were never offered any, but they were happy to keep their distance from the horses. When these treats were produced the giants would bite and kick out at each other.

Rumpy and Dumpy wanted none of that. They had seen such behaviour before. Now and again strangers would walk along the narrow road and stop at the fence to call the horses. Whatever they produced from their pockets and gave to the horses, it caused the same behaviour. These strangers had glanced over at Rumpy and Dumpy. One or two had made mooing sounds and laughed, but their main interest was the horses who in exchange for the offerings would allow the strangers to rub their noses. Rumpy and Dumpy shuddered at the thought of any stranger attempting to rub their noses. However, as the weeks went by, and Rumpy and Dumpy had become more confident as regards manoeuvering their way around the giants, they let their curiosity overcome them and when strangers with offerings appeared, they would get as close to the fence as possible, still keeping a healthy distance from the giants.

On the odd occasion a stranger would throw a white cube down for them. One sniff of the cube was all they needed to confirm their opinion of the giants, namely that they were mad, out of their minds, insane. How could they fight over, let alone eat something that had no familiar, delicious smell. The horses were more than pleased when Rumpy and Dumpy showed no interest in these white cubes. This confirmed their belief that all cattle were dumb animals. How wrong the horses were! The young couple who visited the horses once a month would soon be teaching those giants a lesson.

They had begun their monthly visits before Arine was born. At that time Atropa and Speedy shared the field with the chestnut mare, Gina, and the two Yaks. They always brought carrots and bread for the horses. They would have fed the Yaks, but they never came over to the fence. When the Jersey cows arrived, the couple offered them titbits, but they showed no interest. They had yet to meet the new pair.

They were just passing the stables on their way to the horses, when they saw Rumpy and Dumpy emerge. Their first thought was, "Aren't they beautiful." Then it hit them that these two must have replaced the Jersey cows. That saddened the couple, as they had grown fond of the Jerseys. Most visitors to the field only had eyes for the horses. But they had had eyes and comforting words for the Jerseys, too. They greeted the new arrivals and from the plastic bag they were carrying they produced some bread. They crouched down and held out the bread in their hands. Rumpy and Dumpy were not going to be lured by such tactics. They were not as stupid as the giants. They sniffed the air, trying to make out what was being offered to them. They could see it had no resemblance to the white cubes the horses went mad for. The young couple threw the bread down at their feet and both Rumpy and Dumpy jumped back in fright.

They decided to leave the new arrivals to explore the wonders of bread, and off they marched down the narrow road to the horses. Already the sound of the plastic bag alerted the horses to the presence of visitors and food. They ran to meet their callers and positioned themselves at the fence. Dumpy and Rumpy had moved round to the gate at the top of the field and were watching. The horses devoured their bread and carrots with no biting or kicking this time. The couple rubbed the horses' noses and then saying goodbye they turned to walk up the road. Rumpy and Dumpy continued to stand near the gate. The young couple threw two carrots over the gate for them and, after initial hesitation and much sniffing, Rumpy and Dumpy took them in their mouths and marvelled at the taste of this new food. Happy to see these animals enjoying their gifts, the couple took their leave and headed past the stables. The bread they had thrown to the new arrivals was gone, so bread and carrots would now be on the menu for Rumpy and Dumpy too. Two weeks later when the couple returned, the Highlanders were at the top of the field and the horses were down at the bottom. The visitors crouched down, as if trying to make themselves smaller than Rumpy and Dumpy. Again they held out their offerings, but Rumpy and Dumpy were not to be lured to the fence. They had every reason to be afraid of people. People had wrenched them away from their mothers and their herd. People had barricaded them in their stable. People were not to be trusted.

Again the couple threw their offerings down. As Rumpy and Dumpy enjoyed their titbits their would-be friends talked to them. Of course the new arrivals could not comprehend what the young couple were saying, but they liked the sounds. They liked being given their treats before the horses had a chance to snatch them. Had the giants not been far away at the bottom of the field, there would have been no titbits for them. The sound of a plastic bag would have brought the horses racing to fight over the tasty morsels. Rumpy and Dumpy were well aware of that and were grateful. Again the couple made their way down to the horses, calling out their names. Just as before, on their way back the pair tossed the last bits of bread over the fence for Rumpy and Dumpy and saying good-bye they disappeared round the corner.

Two visits from the young couple were enough to make Rumpy and Dumpy understand why the horses displayed such undignified behaviour when competing for titbits. Unlike the white cubes, these offerings were very tasty morsels indeed, so tasty that, yes, should the occasion arise, they too would be prepared to fight off the horses for such treats. They didn't reckon on such an occasion, as the young couple had been the only visitors since the really cold weather set in. They continued to be the only visitors throughout the cold winter.

One day the couple arrived to find the horses a bit too close to Rumpy and Dumpy for peaceful feeding, so they began walking back in the direction of the stables, calling out for Rumpy and Dumpy to follow. Rumpy and Dumpy walked up to the stable where, hidden from the horses' view, they tucked into their bread and carrots. By now they knew their names, names given to them by these visitors. They quite enjoyed having names. The giants had names, the dogs who came by in tow had names. People give all beings names, it seems.

Rumpy and Dumpy knew all the regular dogs not only by sight but also by name. There was Flop-ear-sit-down, Dino-come-on, Trina-stop-that, Asterix-you-naughty-boy, and Maydel-come-here. Well, now they had names, too. They also knew the young couple's names. He was Illy and she was Sarah. Come snow or rain Illy and Sarah continued their visits. There were times when peaceful feeding was inhibited by the giants, but then Sarah would start feeding the giants and Illy would lead Rumpy and Dumpy away for their morsels. Now Rumpy and Dumpy ate from Illy's or Sarah's hand. The young couple had given them no reason to continue their policy of distrust and, with the ground so wet and soggy, morsels taken from a hand didn't get mud on them. Morsels from the hand reached their mouths alone, unlike morsels on the ground, which immediately brought out the giants' fighting spirit.

TWO

PARADISE LOST

Winter passed by, and spring began to bring everything to life – including visitors to the field. The sound of plastic bags not only alerted the horses but also Rumpy and Dumpy, who now competed with the giants for treats. The horses always got the lion's share of the goodies and always allowed the visitors to rub their noses. Rumpy and Dumpy were not going to sink to or risk such practices. Still, Rumpy and Dumpy always managed to get the odd piece of bread or carrot, which was well worth waiting for. White cubes of sugar were always left to the giants. As visitors got used to the fact that Rumpy and Dumpy loved bread and carrots and apples, they used their offerings to get the two close to the fence. Some did this out of interest; others just wanted to tug at Rumpy's and Dumpy's horns. If they managed one tug, they certainly didn't manage a second, for Rumpy and Dumpy wielded their horns like clubs and chopping the air they brought them down heavily on the offending hand. They were not to be confused with the giants. Tasty food or no tasty food, they were not going to tolerate such liberties; Sarah and Illy were allowed to stroke their horns and no one else. Trust had to be earned, not bought. It was nothing new to Rumpy and Dumpy that people might not behave decently. Some strangers would hit them with sticks or if Rumpy and Dumpy were further away from the fence, they would throw sticks and stones at them. The boy who lived next to the museum liked to taunt them with lighted matches and branches from the forest. He, unfortunately, was a regular visitor. When Farmer Little or Sarah and Illy were at the field, he would try to behave himself. They had scolded him more than once because of his antics. But as soon as they left, the tormentor in him drove the animals away in fear. Rumpy and Dumpy encountered other children as well as adults like him, too.

They learnt that, apart from the tormentor, the regular visitors were the ones who behaved decently. There was Danny and his dog, Rolly, and Danny's parents. There was Mrs Rose and her dog, Trixie. They came once a week and, like Sarah and Illy, they fed Rumpy and Dumpy first, then the giants. Rolly and Trixie, who would turn their noses up at stale bread at home, always begged to partake of a morsel of stale bread when Rumpy and Dumpy were being fed. Like Sarah and Illy, Danny, his parents and Mrs. Rose would talk to Rumpy and Dumpy for a long time. Yes, they were decent folk. So was Mr. Scratchback, who rode to the field on his bicycle several times a week. In the beginning he only brought himself, but no food. But he'd stand and talk to Rumpy and Dumpy and one day he produced a long piece of wood from near the fence and tried to scratch their backs with it. Rumpy and Dumpy had seen sticks before and they flew back from the fence. But as time passed they began to trust this visitor and they accepted his services of back scratching gratefully. He scratched those parts their horns could not reach, and how often they had wished they could scratch those itchy parts. Yes, his services were more than welcome, as were the ears of corn he would begin collecting from the fields on his ride over to Rumpy and Dumpy. These were the regular, decent visitors.

Spring was wonderful in yet another way. One day Farmer Little came to the field with Crystal. The gate was left open and the horses were led out of the field. At first Rumpy and Dumpy were agitated. They didn't like change, and they didn't know what was happening. Admittedly the giants had taunted, kicked, and bitten them, but the giants were the only herd Rumpy and Dumpy had. Both the Highlanders and the horses were, after all, herd animals. The gate was closed and the horses were led down the narrow road. Rumpy and Dumpy followed them along the fence next to the road.

At the bottom of Rumpy's and Dumpy's field there was another little field with a small space in between. Crystal and Farmer Little led the horses into the small field, a really tiny enclosure in comparison to the one they were used to, and they left the horses there. Relieved that their herd was only next door, Rumpy and Dumpy spent the rest of the day in view of the horses. They nibbled at the grass and looked over every now and again to see what the giants were doing. The horses were not very happy about this new development but they accepted it. They trusted Farmer Little and Crystal, so they would just have to stay put and, well, it would only be for a short while anyway, the horses thought.

Now Rumpy and Dumpy had utter peace and quiet. No teasing, no kicking, no biting. Their growing, shiny horns had often struck out at the giants' flanks, but such painful blows had never caused the horses to run away or stop their antics. The horses now encountered Rumpy and Dumpy with a healthy respect for their horns and Dumpy at least would stand his ground when the giants' antics began. But now there were no antics – there was no having to wait to use the water fountain in the giants' stable. Indeed the giants' stable became their stable, for it was much bigger than their own. Now there was undisturbed feeding when Sarah and Illy or the regulars came to visit. In short, Rumpy and Dumpy had landed in heaven, in paradise. Rumpy and Dumpy now relaxed as never before. Now the field was *their* playground and, running like the wind, they chased each other, kicking out at the sun with their hind legs. Dumpy loved showing off how he could come to a sudden sliding standstill. They licked each other's ears and eyes and took their naps under the tree in front of the giants' stable. Spring had brought good weather, and the grass and leaves were busy weaving their carpet of green in the sunlight.

Watching Rumpy and Dumpy together, it became very clear to Sarah and Illy that their bovine friends had begun a new relationship. Like young lovebirds they treasured every moment together on their paradise island. They were seldom to be found down at the bottom of the field in view of the horses. They had each other for company. More they did not need or wish for. Farmer Little came by only now and again. Crystal always went to the tiny field, to the giants. While the horses had Crystal, Rumpy and Dumpy had Sarah and Illy.

This heavenly situation went on for weeks, indeed months. Sometimes the horses were taken off in a trailer. They were always brought back the same day or the next day and returned to the tiny field. Rumpy and Dumpy would have been happy to keep everything the way it was now. Spring had turned to summer and they had luscious grass and leaves in abundance. The day the giants were led back to the big field, they pounded their joy into the earth as they raced up and down. Rumpy and Dumpy raced with them, relishing the joy of running with the herd.

Only after the race had ended as spontaneously as it had begun did Rumpy and Dumpy realise that the giants had pounded back their ownership into every blade of grass, sending Rumpy's and Dumpy's paradise reeling up to the skies. Now that the giants were back in residence, Crystal and her friend, Sue, often spent the long summer evenings riding around the big field. As ever Crystal rode Atropa, and Sue rode Speedy. Sarah and Illy would often appear in the middle of such events, and that made Rumpy and Dumpy doubly happy. They could munch on their favourite treats. They could stand at the fence and enjoy their friends' company, their backs turned to the somewhat unnerving movement and speed of the giants. And they could show Crystal that two people had earned their trust. Only these friends were allowed to stroke their horns, and when these special visitors called, Rumpy and Dumpy followed. Crystal, who was indeed amazed, began a conversation with Sarah and Illy. What had always been very clear to Rumpy and Dumpy soon became very clear to Sarah and Illy in the course of this conversation. Crystal did not particularly care for cattle.

Her father had always had two on the field, hoping cattle would eat the weeds the horses won't touch. In her eyes you couldn't strike up a relationship with cattle. She believed they were not very intelligent or sensitive.

"Now horses move out of the way when you want them to," she said. "They understand. Cattle only move when you give them a reminder, namely a kick in the stomach. Of course it doesn't hurt them. They are built like tanks. The horses need the odd kick now and again, too. But they understand. They are loving, yet independent. They are capable of learning when to trot, to gallop, to move sideways, backwards. They know how to perform at shows and competitions." *Yes,* Sarah and Illy thought, the whip had taught those horses a lot.

Sarah and Illy often came upon Crystal at the field and talked with her. They got to know Crystal's friend, Sue, too. Sue was somewhat afraid of Dumpy. He was now becoming a massive, magnificent bull and he liked to make his voice heard when necessary. His bellow was not only loud but to Sue it was unnerving. Crystal made it very clear that she was the boss in that field, and so Sue only entered when Crystal was there too. Sue's boyfriend, Roy, did not share his girlfriend's fears. Indeed the day Sarah and Illy first saw him, he was in the field, confidently striding over to the horses with an enormous plastic bag full of stale bread rolls. The sight of the plastic bag drew Rumpy and Dumpy in his wake. He fed the horses and Rumpy and Dumpy waited patiently for their portion. They were used to the horses getting the lion's share, but surely there would be the odd roll for them. Roy threw a roll to Rumpy and Dumpy, but Dumpy's was quickly gobbled up by Arine. Rumpy snatched hers just in time and munched away to Dumpy's dismay. Where was his? Roy continued to feed the horses and Dumpy began to bellow. By now Illy and Sarah were standing at the fence. Roy had spectators. He turned to Dumpy, saying, "In a minute. Wait!" Dumpy waited but as the contents of the enormous bag dwindled, his bellow became louder and more piercing.

Whether Dumpy's behaviour had not merited a roll, or Roy had forgotten his promise, the bag was empty and Roy turned to walk to the gate and leave. Dumpy continued to bellow and as Roy strode off, he strode after him. Fair is fair – he hadn't had his roll yet. Rumpy remained where she was, but not Dumpy. No doubt having Sarah and Illy as spectators did not make Roy any happier about this development. Roy turned to find Dumpy right behind him. It was still quite a way to the gate and Roy was not happy. Panic struck and Roy dashed to the fence and clambered over onto the road close to where Illy and Sarah were standing.

They sympathised with Dumpy's disappointment. Hadn't he been bellowing his indignation to the whole world? They tried to make it clear to Roy that Dumpy's "bark was worse than his bite." Roy laughed the situation off, though he did not convince Sarah and Illy. Farmer Little's reaction to the episode was more convincing. Sarah and Illy bumped into him at the field a week later and he really did laugh at Roy's dash for the fence. How hollow the ring of that laughter sounded in their ears, when the following week Crystal told them that Dumpy would be leaving the field. Well, Dumpy was just too big and he had become too aggressive. The episode with Roy proved that. And Dumpy had served his purpose. Rumpy was sure to have a calf the following spring.

Suddenly Sarah and Illy understood why Rumpy and Dumpy had been separated from the horses for those months of paradise, now lost forever. Sarah and Illy wanted to know where Dumpy would be going. They had not reckoned with Crystal's matter-of-fact answer.

"The slaughterhouse, of course. He's eighteen months old. That's the right age to get a good price for his meat." Sarah and Illy were devastated. Dumpy to be slaughtered! And Rumpy? Was she to be left to the whims of the giants all on her own, without her protector and friend? Sarah and Illy would have to do something. They asked when Dumpy was to be picked up.

"Tomorrow morning, it's all arranged," Crystal answered, and with that she looked at her watch and said she would have to get back home. Speechless – Sarah and Illy were utterly speechless. They thought of Dumpy's fate. They thought of Rumpy. They thought of Dumpy's and Rumpy's calf due in spring. Dumpy would never see that calf, never see Rumpy again. Rumpy would have to spend six months alone with the giants. Then she would have to bear her calf and, as well as having to protect herself, she would have to protect her calf. But Dumpy was to be slaughtered in less than twenty-four hours.

Why hadn't they stopped Crystal from leaving? Why hadn't they offered to buy Dumpy – making an offer to buy him could have bought them and Dumpy time? Of course they had no field to put him in. Of course they didn't know how to go about such things. They were city people. Of course they didn't know how much Farmer Little would want for Dumpy or if they could afford his price. But why didn't they just make the offer? This question plagued them all the way home and back to the field again. They couldn't do anything now. They didn't know where Farmer Little lived – no telephone number, nothing. They had gone home to think and at home they knew they had missed their chance of trying to do something. They packed a bag full of goodies and made their way back to the field. They were bringing Dumpy his last supper. It seemed that Rumpy sensed that too. Could she read the signs of Sarah's and Illy's feelings? It certainly appeared that way. She had always been ravenous for their tasty morsels, but this time she refused the tasty titbits and left them all for Dumpy, who was by no means put out at having to eat everything himself. He was his normal self, but not Rumpy.

The following day Sarah and Illy rushed over to the field after work to visit Rumpy. She was standing at the gate all on her own, standing waiting for Dumpy to return. For weeks she waited at that gate. Every day Sarah and Illy visited her and every day she was there. She then took to standing at the fence facing the forest. She would stand there with her back to the gate and to "their" island, staring into the forest. The trees had all shed their leaves and, starved and naked, they stared back at one starved and naked cow. For months she stood at that fence. Through wind, rain, snow, and gales she stood there. When Sarah and Illy came, they would call to her and she would leave her post to feed, but she was distant even with them and she always returned to her spot at the fence once they were gone.

As the months passed by the calf grew within her. Dumpy's calf, new life! During those long winter months there was no life in her spirit. It had fallen from her like the leaves from the trees. A spark was rekindled for a short while, when the first snow fell. As the snow swept down, Sarah and Illy arrived in time to witness the most heartrending sight. Rumpy was out in the field all alone, kicking the snowflakes with her back hooves and dancing – a sweet, brief burst of joy, like a child reeling in his first taste of snow. Then she returned to the fence and the forest and her vigil, waiting for spring and her calf, for something to love again, for she knew Dumpy would not return – she knew.

THREE

BOBO

Spring came and awakened life all around. Spring came and greeted the life Rumpy and Dumpy had shared, the birth of their bull calf, Bobo. Illy and Sarah always chose the names and they christened Rumpy's calf Bobo McDump. Bobo was his mother's joy and as much a joy to Sarah and Illy, who had so long waited for Rumpy's months of loneliness to come to an end. Now there were two. There had always been two, just the right number of cattle to keep the pasture clear of nettles – another reason, no doubt, why Dumpy had had to go. Well, it was two again, and thank God for that. It was two again – a bull and a cow.

This time it would remain these two, these two together. Sarah and Illy had made their decision. Dumpy's son was not going to have to face his father's fate. Rumpy was not going to be put through that again. They had made their decision. They would be prepared, they would get everything organised well in advance. But for now they would concentrate on getting to know this new personality, Master Bobo McDump.

Bobo McDump became the star attraction for the visitors to the field. They now brought extra titbits for Rumpy in the hope that her calf would join her at the fence. Everyone wanted to see him up close, this bundle of golden orange fur with blue eyes and long, long eyelashes. He looked like a very large cuddly toy and they all wanted to cuddle him with their eyes at least. He did look sweet and vulnerable. Vulnerable he was, so he generally kept close to the fence next to the forest. There he would spend most of his time sleeping. Rumpy would go off to nibble grass, assured her calf would stay put, well away from any harm. After such feeding bouts she would return to her calf to lick his coat clean with her comforting tongue, and join him for a little nap. Every time he awakened, Bobo would seek out his mother's udder and give it a mighty bash with his head to start the milk flowing. Then he would fill his stomach with milky contentment until he was drowsy from so much drinking and would lie down to sleep again. This being his routine, few visitors got to see him close up. Well, most of them only came by now and again. The regulars were luckier in this respect, as were Sarah and Illy, who visited the field every day after work. When they arrived, Rumpy always came to the fence, and if Bobo was not curled up in a ball sleeping somewhere out of sight, he joined his mother and marvelled at what she allowed these two strangers to do with her – put things in her mouth, stroke her face and shoulders and even her horns. Overcome by curiosity he would sniff at her mouth, wondering what the strangers had given her. He would then sniff at her face and horns trying to recognize some familiar smell, but neither mouth, face, nor horn offered any smell familiar to Bobo. His quest unsuccessful, he would usually turn to Rumpy's udder, filling his nose with her familiar smells and his stomach with milky protection, for though his mother associated with this strange human breed, he was not happy with their unfamiliar smells, their quick movements, particularly their flapping hands. All that frightened him. He sought comfort, and his mother had that in abundance – her milk, her sweet scent, her rough tongue brushing his coat, leaving him in a cocoon of warm, protective saliva.

There were many things the calf had to get used to in his new world. There were the horses, who, for the first few weeks at least, left Rumpy and Bobo in peace. There was Farmer Little and his daughter Crystal. There were the local dogs. There were the noisy cars and tractors that ploughed their way along the narrow road. There was the boy who lived next to the museum. All these new aspects of life at the field frightened him. That noisy monster, the tractor, filled him with panic and put him to flight. The fact that his mother showed no fear of the tractor did not instill any calm in Bobo. But gradually her reactions became his. He encountered the local dogs, the boy from next door, Farmer Little and Crystal with a healthy sense of caution. He was even more cautious when the horses were close by. Sarah's and Illy's visits were met with calm. But the tractor remained a monster and he always ran. Only one thing caused such panic in his mother – the sight of a trailer. So trailers were also monsters in this new world.

With everything else he felt at home, with the birds and the rabbits and the ducks from the nearby pond. As the weeks passed, his world expanded in ever-widening circles as his fast legs spun around the figure of his mother grazing peacefully. Running round and round her, he would flick his hind legs into the air, first one, then another. His efforts drew a smile from Sarah and Illy, who were endlessly entertained by watching this beginner teach himself the art of kicking. Elated by his success, Bobo would repeat his kicks again and again. He was ever keen to show his mother that he was a fine bull worthy of her pride. Practice makes perfect and soon Bobo learnt the thrill of kicking the air with both hooves. Yes, he was a fine bull and though he had no horns that were visible to the outside world, he had his long imaginary horns, as long as mother's horns, almost. So when Rumpy joined in his playtime activities, he would press his head against her neck, pushing and parrying with those giant horns of his. Rumpy would gently push and parry back. He would feel her horns gently brushing against his fur and would change position for a new attack. Such games would strengthen his neck muscles, muscles he would need later to push and parry effectively to protect himself. Rumpy was his protector now and would be for some time to come, but, like his father Dumpy, one day he would have to protect Rumpy and himself.

Bobo was two months old when Atropa had her stallion foal, Dragon. At birth Dragon stood taller then Bobo. He could run as fast as Bobo, and could fly around the field, whereas Bobo was only an excellent runner over short distances. Dragon and Bobo were soon drawn to each other.

Mothers played for a while, but then they would go off to graze or have a nap. They weren't serious playmates who could play and play for hours. So Dragon and Bobo became playmates. Dragon loved chasing Bobo around the field. When Bobo could run no more, he would stop, turn, and with his head lowered he would begin to push at Dragon's flanks, parrying with his imaginary horns, which now were little stublets peeking out from his orange fur. Dragon would lower his head and nip Bobo's ears and shoulders – all in fun.

Still, when the biting got too much for Bobo, he would run off to the protective "skirts" of his mother. He never stayed there for too long, but would go bounding back over towards his pal. The horses and Rumpy left the youngsters to play, but in the evenings the horses would play their chasing games with Rumpy and Bobo, and in these games the two playmates were on opposite sides. Rumpy hated the chase and always headed for the stable. Bobo joined her in retreat. He was not big enough to put those horses to flight yet, but time was on his side. Despite these evening antics, the two youngsters spent their playtime together, returning to their own kind only for nourishing milk, grooming or a nap. Bobo had acquired a pal, and though the rules his friend played by were different from Bobo's rules, they played and that was what mattered.

FOUR

BULLY, BULLY, BULLY, BULLY, COME, COME, COME, COME

Slowly, gradually, Bobo made friends with Sarah and Illy. When called he would join his mother at the fence, and there he would nibble on his carrot while his mother chewed her way through the rest of the goodies. Then he and his mother would stand like statues enjoying hands that scratched and rubbed their shoulders, their ears, their necks and the backs of their horns. Bobo particularly delighted in using an outstretched palm as something to butt. That game was not encouraged, as Illy and Sarah were well aware that Bobo should not play "games" with people. He could play games with his mother and with Dragon, but people were too fragile for any games with a growing bull. And grow he did that summer. His horns became truly visible. His orange fur was replaced by a long, shiny coat of every reddish hue along with blonde and black streaks. His legs and his shoulders became sturdier and his stomach rounder. He was no longer a calf but a young bull.

That summer his circle of accepted visitors grew, too. He got to know and accept all the regulars: Mrs. Rose and Trixie, Danny and his parents, Rolly, and Mr. and Mrs. Scratchback. When they arrived with titbits he would join his mother at the fence and wait for his goodies to be thrown on the ground. The regulars often came by when Sarah and Illy were there. Their topic of conversation was always the same – Rumpy and Bobo. The regulars always marvelled at how Rumpy and Bobo stood like statues for their grooming. Rumpy would allow Mr. Scratchback to scratch her back with his stick, but no one was allowed to touch them except the young couple. Mr. Scratchback often tried to stroke Rumpy's horns but she made it quite clear she preferred his stick. So in the end he respected her wishes. He was a grey-haired pensioner with a zest for life and he entertained Sarah and Illy with his anecdotes. What also entertained them was the fact that he would cycle over to the field via the cornfields and, like a young lad, he would fill his pockets and bag with ears of corn, keeping an eye out, lest the farmer should catch him. Rumpy and Bobo adored corn and Mr. Scratchback loved giving them their favourite food and talking to them. What entertained Sarah and Illy most about Mr. Scratchback was how he would call Bobo to the fence. In a singing tone he would chant, "Bully, bully, bully, bully, come, come, come, come." He chanted for as long as it took Bobo to reach the fence.

Sarah and Illy often spent the long summer evenings at the field talking to Farmer Little and Crystal. They were well aware of the young couple's feelings for Rumpy and Bobo, and of Rumpy's and Bobo's attachment to the young couple. Rumpy and Bobo never strayed off when Sarah and Illy were talking to the Littles. They waited for a comforting scratch or rub and they always got them. Indeed they seemed to show off at such times, as if to say, "Look what our friends are allowed to do!" The couple's conversations with the Littles were always about Rumpy and Bobo and the horses. Farmer Little had a soft spot for Rumpy and Bobo. Sarah and Illy were pleased about that. Though Farmer Little owned them, he knew that the cattle "belonged" to the young couple in some special way. He did not have the time to build up a relationship like that with Rumpy and Bobo, so he enjoyed observing this bond with these special two-legged friends. Crystal found Bobo entertaining, particularly in his playtime activities with Dragon, who was Crystal's pride and joy along with Atropa. She spoke of her dreams of taking Dragon off to shows. She was sure he would grow to be a winner. Sarah and Illy were happy that Crystal found Bobo entertaining, though they wondered how she would feel once Bobo was bigger, as big as his father, Dumpy. Now that they got on with the Littles and saw them regularly, they knew there would come a time to discuss the future of Bobo and Rumpy. This time they would be ready to rescue their beloved bull.

They were determined to intervene in any plans that would prevent their friends from enjoying a full life. This time they would make their own plans to secure Bobo's future and Rumpy's too. Rumpy was a truly independent spirit. Hardship had taught her to rely on her own strength and her wits – they were always at hand. She had now come to trust that Sarah and Illy would also be there to keep her safe.

FIVE

THE KEY
TO THE GATE

The long summer nights became memories. By autumn Bobo and Dragon were certainly bigger boys who still loved to play. Rumpy was not so enamoured of Dragon as Bobo was. When the horses began their chasing and biting games, Dragon would join in the biting as much as the others. "How dare such a youngster forget his station in life? He needs to be taught a lesson." Rumpy thought. And from then on when Bobo and Dragon were playing, Rumpy would often seize her opportunity and dart off to Dragon, give him a whack with her horns before darting back to safety. It was always Bobo who then received the bites Dragon intended for Rumpy. But Bobo enjoyed his friend's antics and now he was so much bigger and stronger that he could ward off many a bite with his pushing and parrying and spinning round on the spot.

Even with the other horses he was more confident about standing his ground when the chasing games began. He got many a kick from Atropa and Arine, but he continued to establish himself as a fighter and not a bull who retreats to the stable. When Crystal began training Dragon on the long rope, with her long whip in hand, Bobo wanted to join in the new game. Again he had to learn that there could be no games when people were involved. He left Dragon to his training and went off to nibble.

About this time Crystal invited the young couple to go into the field and enjoy their friends from the other side of the fence. Illy was in like a shot, but Sarah suddenly felt squeamish. She was a city girl. Yes, she loved her friends and the horses, too. But having so many large bodies around her plus the fear of them engaging in chasing games turned her legs to jelly. Illy reassured her, and so sticking close to his side she entered the field. Rumpy immediately approached the two and gently tapping Illy's hand with her horn, requested neck rubs. The sight of Rumpy's horn aiming in the direction of Illy's hand put Sarah to flight. Outside she turned to see Illy rubbing Rumpy's neck and had to laugh at her own timidity. By the time she was at Illy's and Rumpy's side, Bobo was just arriving. He was a size Sarah could emotionally deal with on this first direct encounter, and so she stretched out her hands and gave him neck rubs and shoulder rubs. Then Dragon came over to say hello to the couple who always brought treats for him and the other horses. Sarah gave him nose rubs and shoulder rubs. Bobo did not want intruders. He pushed at Dragon, who then moved over to Crystal. Then Bobo rubbed his head against Sarah's leg. She turned so quickly that he jumped back and with his head down began his parrying movements. She was not going to panic and run again. She turned to Illy. "You frightened him, turning so quickly. Just walk round to the side of him and pat his back." Sarah did exactly that, and Bobo stood like a statue for his cuddles. Then Rumpy walked over to Sarah for her stroking while Illy tended to Bobo. It certainly was more enjoyable having cuddles this side of the fence. Now Sarah and Illy could rub their backs and their flanks. Sarah and Illy were as happy as Rumpy and Bobo.

Imagine the young couple's joy when a week later Farmer Little gave them a key to the side gate positioned directly in front of Rumpy's and Bobo's stable. They were such ardent visitors, he decided they should have a key and visit the animals whenever they wished. Now the regulars always saw the two of them in the field brushing Rumpy and Bobo. The horses were groomed with brushes, now they were, too. Their brushes were firm and rough and as they were being pulled through their long shiny coats, they felt like their own tongues, when they licked each other's fur. No fence between them now and no fence to their future together now that Farmer Little had given them the key. They couldn't believe their luck and the generosity of the Little family. Their motive, however, soon became clear.

Three weeks later Crystal announced that Bobo would be sent to the slaughterhouse before Christmas. Bobo was getting bigger. They didn't want to have the same problems they had had with Dumpy as he grew bigger and stronger. Rumpy could be artificially inseminated. That way she could have a calf every year. It was a shock to hear that this plan to seal Bobo's doom was already in place! The gallows again – so soon! The young couple would never let this happen. They had made their decision a year ago, and this time they did not hesitate. They told Crystal they were quite prepared to buy Bobo. Their only problem was where they would find a field for him. Of course they hadn't forgotten Rumpy in their plans, but once they had found a field, they would purchase her freedom, too.

One week later Sarah and Illy were invited to the Littles' home and as they were served coffee they were presented with a contract. It was not a sales contract but a contract for board and keep. Bobo could stay in the field, but the couple would have to pay for his upkeep. They could feed Rumpy and Bobo themselves if they wished. Should Bobo need to be slaughtered at some point, they would get a percentage of the money for his meat. The young couple signed, happy that they now had an official hand in Bobo's future, yet somehow sensing that the Littles were only out to make money out of them as the monthly fee for Bobo's keep was by no means paltry. They would need to look ahead for another field and the money to buy Bobo and Rumpy. It was time to make serious preparations. Yes, the young couple were naive, but their naiveté was the key to Bobo's and Rumpy's survival.

Sarah and Illy took on the daily feeding of Rumpy and Bobo. Rumpy's pellets were placed in the trough in her stable, while Bobo's were put in a bucket and given to him outside the horses' stable. This physical separation at feeding time proved to be the ideal solution. Rumpy always devoured her pellets in no time and knowing Bobo was still a slow eater in comparison, she would immediately be after his portion, so distance was vital. While Bobo was still nibbling on his pellets, Illy would distract Rumpy. Then fresh hay was placed in the feeder and fresh straw put down in their stable. The horses put up with this new arrangement and at first showed little interest in the young couple. They knew Crystal would be along later to feed them and spoil them. When Crystal arrived, the young couple were often still at the field. It was on such an occasion that Crystal suggested that they train Bobo to walk on a lead. She could lend them one of Dragon's halters.

Sarah and Illy considered this suggestion and both agreed that if they could train Bobo to walk with them while he was still young, that would certainly be a help later. They wanted eventually to have him in a field of their own. To get to that field he would have to walk into a trailer. This would be a lot easier if they could lead Bobo up the ramp. Crystal brought the halter and showed Sarah and Illy how to put it on. Bobo didn't seem too bothered about the halter; neither did Rumpy. The young couple were more anxious as they were afraid the halter could get caught in the fence. Still they proceeded with the plan and each day they would attach a rope to the halter and try to encourage Bobo to walk with them. Bobo didn't really go along with their tentative attempts at training him. He wasn't happy.

Seeing his frustration and feeling rather frustrated themselves, the young couple gave up the project and removed the halter. Bobo always came when he was called. He always obeyed when he was told to stop any forbidden antics – pushing and parrying games being the main taboo activity. They truly believed they could train him in their own way. Their voice commands had worked up till now. One "STOP!" from Illy always brought Bobo to a halt. Immediately Bobo would lick Illy's hand, as if to say, "I'm sorry, I forgot myself." Then he would stand like a statue waiting for Illy's comforting rubs. Yes, it was Illy who Bobo sought as a prospective playmate. With Sarah, Bobo was particularly gentle and calm. Bobo obviously sensed that Illy was much more confident handling him and his mother than Sarah was.

After feeding and grooming their bovine friends, the young couple would often walk with them while they nibbled on what bits of grass they could find. Perhaps out of jealousy, the horses would gallop at full speed in the cattle's direction. Rumpy and Bobo would race over to the young couple and hide behind them. The first time this happened Sarah thought she was going to faint, but Illy told her to keep calm and stand absolutely still. Sarah dreamed of racing to the fence but she did stand still and the horses literally brushed past them with only inches to spare. "Why run to us?" Sarah asked Illy. They had always run to the stable before. Illy was well aware that the two now saw Sarah and Illy as their protectors, and he was right. When alarmed by the horses, strange dogs or hunters' guns in the distance, Bobo and Rumpy always positioned themselves next to or behind their protectors. Sarah gained more and more confidence in this new role and though her heart was always in her mouth when Bobo and Rumpy raced towards them, she knew all would be well, and it always was. She stood just as still when one day Atropa and Arine raced towards her and Illy, as if using them as slalom poles. In time, the horses gave up their intimidation practices and accepted the young couple's right to go about their business without hindrance.

Though Bobo was taking on manly proportions, he would not forego having his fill of his mother's warm milk. Rumpy tried hard to put a stop to Bobo's feeding. She would kick out with her hind legs and move off as soon as his head came close to her udder, but he was so persistant that she always gave in. It wasn't easy for Bobo to get his head positioned under Rumpy's udder now that he was as big as his mother. But where there's a will, there's a way and Bobo's will, when it came to Rumpy's milk, never dwindled.

Bobo was aware of his growing strength and that strength increased his confidence, too. Up till now the only horse he viewed as a companion was Dragon, his playmate and sparring partner. Now Bobo began seeking the company of Arine, a full grown stallion that appeared to have become Bobo's idol. Whenever it was time for Bobo to chew the cud, he would position himself next to Arine, looking up at the horse as if marvelling at his hero's strength and dimensions.

Arine was the strongest male in Bobo's herd, so it was quite natural for Bobo to see Arine as the "lead bull," the one he would so want to emulate once he was full grown. Amazingly, Arine tolerated this adulation. Nor did Rumpy show any signs of alarm. No doubt she was well aware of how much Bobo was missing out on not having fellow bulls around to play with, to learn from. He only had the two male horses, Dragon and Arine. So he made do with what he had. Now that Arine had come to accept his company, Bobo took to trying to mount his hero. Such familiarity was not met with tolerance but hefty kicks to Bobo's head and neck.

Dragon, on the other hand, saw Bobo's mounting tactics as part of their games, and he would mount Bobo in turn.

Dragon, a far more formidable biter than Bobo, introduced a new game that was not at all to Bobo's liking. In the middle of play Dragon would sink his teeth into Bobo's snout and pull with all his might. Unable to wield his horns with his nose locked in this position, Bobo became Dragon's puppet. Wherever Dragon pulled, Bobo had to follow. It took Bobo a few weeks to learn how to avoid the nose lock. It took much longer for his fur to grow back over the imprint of Dragon's teeth on his nose. Dragon was Bobo's only playmate, so Dragon's antics were always taken in jest.

The chasing and biting games initiated by Atropa never seemed to be in jest. If Sarah and Illy weren't around, Rumpy always headed for the stable, as soon as the giants started the chase. Bobo would now stand his ground and find himself being rammed by Atropa in one direction and Arine in the other direction. He took what they had to give and wielding his horns as they came at him, he showed them he was a force to be dealt with.

Rumpy would look on from the stables. Yes, he was becoming a strong bull, she could see that. And to the young couple's surprise and no doubt Bobo's as well, Rumpy began to initiate outbreaks of chasing and biting. She would incite the horses and then beckon Bobo to come and protect her. He always did as she wished, if somewhat reluctantly, and she would always head for the stable to watch. Were these tests of strength a vital part of his education or Rumpy's way of getting her own back on the giants? The young couple did not know. They guessed it might be both.

SIX

THE RITE
OF SPRING

That winter the couple took on feeding the horses as well as caring for their bull and cow. Just as Rumpy used to steal Bobo's pellets, now Atropa and Arine tried to steal Dragon's feed. Like Bobo, he was a slow eater, which gave the others an opportunity for theft. Illy had to distract Arine and Atropa while Sarah monitored Dragon's progress and kept Rumpy and Bobo out of the horses' stable. They too would have gladly gobbled up Dragon's pellets.

Dragon had known the young couple from birth and unlike the other horses, who walked off down the field as soon as feeding time was over, he liked to hang around with his friend, Bobo for cuddles and games. His favourite sport with Illy and Sarah was trying to bite their shoes or pull at their coats. Rumpy always showed her disapproval of Dragon's hanging around by giving him a whack of her horns. So long as Illy, Sarah and Bobo were nearby, Dragon seldom gave Rumpy the bite he thought she so deserved. Bobo tolerated his playmate more, but he too preferred not to share his friends. He did not however use his horns to make this point clear. He would take his playmate to one side, have a little game with him, then, returning to his two-legged friends, he would make it clear that he had other business to see to. Dragon would then go off reluctantly to join the others.

As the winter turned fierce and cold the horses and Rumpy and Bobo spent most of the time in their stables. Sarah and Illy restricted their visits to feeding and a few cuddles. Bobo was now able to gobble his pellets up quickly, and was big enough to keep Rumpy away from his food, so he got his pellets in his trough in the stable. Sarah and Illy were glad to be able to stand and watch their friends eating indoors. The cold wind didn't bite its way into their stable so easily, and the warmth from the air from Rumpy's and Bobo's nostrils helped to keep the temperature tolerable for a while. In this frigid weather Sarah and Illy gladly buried their cold hands into their friends' long coats to warm their frozen fingers.

Despite the fierce cold and snow and ice there were days when Sarah and Illy arrived at the field to see the horses lined up waiting for Atropa to let them into their stable. She was the queen and she liked to prove it. Even Arine stood patiently, followed by Speedy and of course Dragon right at the end. Luckily Bobo and Rumpy were not subjected to such tactics. Yes, they had to get their water from the horses' stable, but in winter they could lick the snow and drink their fill. They had their own stable, a stable the horses couldn't get into, as it was low to the ground. Dragon could manage to scrape his way into their stable, but he seldom tried when Rumpy was inside, as he had a healthy respect for her horns. Being the smallest of the horses he did take advantage of his size to steal hay from Rumpy's and Bobo's stable when they were out in the field. Equally Rumpy had no qualms about going into the horses' stable for a drink when Dragon was there. Her horns gave her free passage, and just as well they did, for Dragon would make a game of playing with the water fountain. Perhaps he liked the sound of running water, perhaps he liked the power he had to make the water flow for as long as he wanted or perhaps he liked how the metal rubbed against his nose – whatever it was, if Rumpy hadn't had the horns to put him to flight, he would have spent hours and hours letting the water gush over the rim of the water fountain.

That winter the young couple began subscribing to farmers' magazines. They pored over the ads, looking for fields to rent. There were hardly any in their area. Most of them were far away, but they kept looking and hoping. One day there was an article about a veterinarian in the local newspaper, featuring her herd of Scottish Highlanders. There was a picture of her rubbing a cow's neck with the rest of the herd surrounding them. The young couple were very happy to know there was someone with the same interests who lived in one of the nearby towns. In response to their telephone call, they were invited over to visit the herd. Mrs. Paul lived in a big farmhouse with her husband, also a vet, and three children. She had one herd of Highlanders close to the farmhouse and another herd in a field on the other side of town. Even before the young couple rang the doorbell they were confronted by Mrs. Paul's total preoccupation with her Scottish Highlanders, for there above the door, like a family's coat of arms, hung a huge plaque depicting the head of a Scottish Highlander. When Mrs Paul opened the door she was wearing that very same image as a gold charm around her neck. They passed the surgery rooms on the ground floor and mounted the stairs to the Pauls' living quarters. Entering the kitchen the couple were again confronted with every possible image of a long-horned Highlander.

Mrs. Paul was an energetic woman, full of enthusiasm for everything, particularly for her family and her herds. She immediately produced photo albums filled with pictures of both together. While the young couple marvelled at the photos, Mrs. Paul explained who was who. Guinness was her prize bull, so there were pictures of him as a young bull positioned next to her very young children, then pictures of him full grown as well as the more recent photographs. He really was enormous. Would Bobo grow that big? There were pictures of every member of her family with every member of her herd. Sarah and Illy listened eagerly to how and why Mrs. Paul had lost her heart to Scottish Highlanders.

Then Bobo became the topic of conversation and the young couple talked of Rumpy and Dumpy and Bobo. They too had pictures of their friends to show Mrs. Paul. She certainly liked the look of Bobo and she went into what constitutes a good breeding bull. Sarah and Illy spoke of their plans for Bobo and their preparations for finding a field. Mrs Paul confirmed what they already knew, namely, it wasn't easy to find fields to rent in that part of the country. She herself was a member of the Scottish Highland Cattle Society and suggested that the couple consider joining the society too. There were hundreds of members scattered all around the country. They had shows two or three times a year and monthly news bulletins. The couple would be sure to find members who could help them. She would certainly do what she could for them, too.

Then Mrs. Paul led the young couple out to Guinness and his herd. They had never seen a herd of Highlanders before. Watching the animals, they realised how isolated Rumpy and Bobo were. They left Mrs. Paul's with a tremendous feeling of optimism for the future. The very next day they sent off their application for membership in the Scottish Highland Cattle Society and decided that they would certainly keep in touch with that wonderful veterinarian, Mrs. Paul.

Spring came and the couple celebrated Bobo's first birthday. He was becoming a massive, fine bull, though compared to Guinness he was still a youngster. Mrs. Paul had told them that a bull would only be full grown at the age of five. Guinness was now three. Bobo enjoyed his extra birthday goodies, as did Rumpy. They were not just mother and son but also the best of friends.

Admittedly Bobo was sometimes disgruntled when his mother initiated jousting with the horses, but he went into action and showed his mettle and he always seemed proud of his combat technique, which was certainly improving. He became more adept at wielding his horns and placing his blows in vulnerable areas. When dealing with Dragon, he would go into a kneeling position and with his head and horns low to the ground he would concentrate his blows on Dragon's legs. Should the two playmates seem to be losing interest in the "fight," Rumpy would tip-toe over to Dragon at full speed, whack him with her horns, and return to her spot to watch the "match."

Rumpy's initiating and prolonging of such fights brought a turning point in the playmates' relationship and in Rumpy's and Bobo's relationship, too. Bobo still drank his mother's milk, but he was now more a companion than a son. He spent more time with Rumpy than he did with Dragon. By the summer it became clear that Rumpy was testing Bobo as a prospective mate. She had no other suitors and mating with family was not taboo among Highland cattle.

One day Rumpy went mad dog. She danced and kicked the air and chased after Bobo. He was so perturbed and confused by her behaviour that he ran into the horses' stable and stood with his head in the corner. The young couple were there to witness this strange event. They called to Bobo, but he would not come out of the stable. Rumpy continued to play mad dog. The couple went into the horses' stable and after much comforting and petting they managed to get Bobo to show his face at the stable entrance. He glanced over at Rumpy but stayed where he was. He was not going to risk being chased like that again. He remained in that position for the rest of his friends' visit. They, too, were at a loss to explain Rumpy's behaviour. A week later her motives were very apparent indeed. Sarah and Illy arrived at the field to find Bobo pacing behind Rumpy, as if he were glued to her. Where she led, he followed. He had no time to stop or greet the couple and enjoy their affection. He obviously had more important business to see to. This development continued for about a week and then things returned to normal.

At last the summer sun began to blaze down and the young couple took to soaking up the sun with their friends. They could often be seen resting with Bobo and Rumpy. As the animals lay chewing the cud, the couple lay beside them – a herd of four. Yes, the couple were herd members and as such they ignored the unsympathetic looks of passersby, who were convinced these people were insane. Perhaps they were, but the regulars didn't think so. They enjoyed seeing the herd of four and secretly wished they could join the herd – Mr. Scratchback particularly. One dog marcher warned the young couple that a bull was a dangerous animal that could not be trusted. "You will find out the hard way if you persist in such folly." But persist they did.

SEVEN

POISTI

By winter it was obvious that Rumpy was expecting a calf.
And Atropa, after a successful summer visit to a stallion,
was expecting her next foal. Again mathematics loomed
large in the young couple's thoughts. There had always been
two and two only! Mixed with their joy at the thought of a
new addition to the herd was their fear for Bobo's future. He
would soon be two years old. His father had been taken at
the age of eighteen months. Like his father he too had not
succumbed to any intimidation tactics from Crystal. They
did not get along, and Crystal was in no way prepared to let
a bull hamper her freedom of movement around the stables.
If Bobo was in the way, he got kicked. He bellowed his
disapproval and was likened to his father for being obstinate.

One Saturday morning in March Poisti, Rumpy's second
bull calf was born. In anticipation of the birth the young

couple arrived at the field early in the morning. They arrived to find Bobo standing over the the dead body of his son, bellowing from the very depths of his heart, bellowing for the whole world to hear. He would not stop bellowing. Rumpy was standing over at the fence to the forest. The young couple were devastated and were just about to drive home to phone the Littles, when Farmer Little arrived with Crystal. A farmer passing by on his tractor had witnessed the blows which had put an end to Poisti's life and he had immediately phoned Farmer Little. The young couple listened as Farmer Little recounted the course of events. As the farmer was approaching the field he saw Poisti on the ground. Rumpy was licking him. He then got up and was about to take his first sip of Rumpy's sweet milk when Atropa came racing towards them and, lashing out with her hind legs, she struck Poisti to the ground. Seeing Poisti's limp body the farmer knew he was dead.

Questions flooded the young couple's minds. "Why? Was it out of jealousy? Was the number three a break with tradition, which Atropa would not tolerate – for then it would be three horses and three Highlanders. But her foal would put the horses back in the majority. Where had Bobo been, when all this happened? Why hadn't they gone to the field earlier? They could have stopped Atropa. Why? Why?" Bobo's continual bellowing drew their attention away from their questions and to his pain. Rumpy was back at her mourning post, her eyes fixed on the naked trees in the forest. Farmer Little and Crystal wanted to remove Poisti's body and bury it. Would Bobo allow them to? The young couple called to their friends and shook their bag of goodies.

Rumpy remained where she was, but Bobo came bellowing towards the young couple and they fed him and cuddled him and talked to him non-stop. They wished to keep his eyes and attention on them and not on Crystal, who by then was carrying the heavy, limp carcass over to where Rumpy was standing. The young couple were not sure of how Bobo would react if he saw Crystal with Poisti. They certainly didn't want Bobo to do anything that might result in his being removed from the field like his father. Poisti's body was thrown over the fence and a few yards into the forest Farmer Little dug a grave for his body and he was buried there.

Once the Littles had left, the young couple went to Poisti's resting place and marked it with the largest stone they could find in the forest. Bobo walked over to Rumpy's side and watched them. Yes, there had always been two. There were still two. Atropa had seen to that. As Rumpy and Bobo mourned, so did the young couple, Mr Scratchback and the other regulars. Weeks passed by and Rumpy still stood at the fence to the forest, now further down from the spot where her calf lay buried. Bobo would be off nibbling grass but she would always be at the fence. The strangest thing was that Atropa took to joining Rumpy at the fence. There they would stand side by side, something they had never done before. It was a sad sight for Sarah and Illy to see a very pregnant Atropa standing next to a mourning mother. But Rumpy accepted Atropa's presence and did not move away when Atropa joined her at the fence. The young couple looked on amazed and wished they could share the communication the two mothers no doubt exchanged. Was this Atropa's act of contrition? It certainly looked that way. Why was Rumpy so forgiving? At that very spot Atropa shared with Rumpy, Prili, Atropa's new foal was born. She was a lively foal and her liveliness made the young couple miss Poisti even more.

It was about this time that Rumpy and Bobo encountered a new addition to "their" herd, one they certainly hadn't reckoned with. A cat appeared in their stable one day and liking the accommodation, he decided to stay. The young couple were sure that the cat had been put out. They provided him with cat food, forgetting that the cat was thoroughly spoilt in this field with an abundant supply of field mice. They decided to call the cat Brodie, and Brodie soon learnt his name and, like his fellow herd members, came when called. For six weeks Brodie kept Bobo and Rumpy company, sleeping in their stable, walking with them in the field and following them back to have a nap. Brodie was an avid hunter. Unfortunately more mice were slain than were eaten. One landed up between Bobo's hoof. Illy had quite a time trying to get the dead mouse out of that position. While Rumpy and Bobo grazed, Brodie hunted. The horses took little notice of this miniature addition. When Brodie strayed into the horses' stable, it was only to nap on the bales of hay. Whenever the young couple arrived he was out on the path to greet them. He always followed Sarah and loved to be lifted and stroked and placed inside Sarah's jacket for extra warmth and comfort. After six weeks the cat disappeared as mysteriously as he had arrived. Some weeks later they discovered that Brodie belonged to a family on a nearby farm. He had obviously been taking his annual holidays with Bobo and Rumpy.

Just after Brodie left, Rumpy and Bobo were in their mating phase again. Unfortunately Sarah and Illy were unaware of this as Bobo did not pace behind Rumpy or ignore them as he had done in the past. Unaware of the situation, Illy was brushing Rumpy while Sarah brushed Bobo. Just as Illy was bent over brushing Rumpy's hind leg, Bobo stepped forward and with his nose pushed Illy away, as if to say "move somewhere else. You can't be here now." Unfortunately Illy, totally off guard, fell and broke his wrist.

Bobo and Rumpy looked on in shock. Rumpy then retreated to the horses' stable leaving Bobo standing stunned, as Sarah scolded him. The dog marcher's warning rang in Sarah's ears, but she had seen what had happened – it was a harmless nudge. Had Illy been upright, the consequences would have been harmless.

Realising the extent of the injury, the pair rushed off to the hospital in their car. Bobo just stood amazed, unable to grasp what had happened or why his friends had rushed off without a good-bye. Hours later the young couple returned to the field, Illy now brandishing an arm and hand in plaster. Bobo saw the gleaming white of the plaster as the young couple walked towards him. As Illy spoke, Bobo began to make such mournful sounds, sounds the young couple had never heard before. Rumpy popped her head out of the horses' stable and then came out to see what was happening.

Sarah and Illy had had enough time to think about and discuss the events while they had been waiting in the hospital. They were sure that Rumpy would be expecting a calf the following spring and they were right, but much was to happen before the next calf was due.

Soon after the incident Crystal told the couple that they wanted Bobo out of the field. If Sarah and Illy wanted to buy him, all well and good, if not then it would be the slaughterhouse. Mathematics was doing its work again. There had always only been two – a calf would set that right. Bobo was now two years old, the right time for a good price for his meat. The young couple immediately got in touch with Mrs Paul. She had helped them when Bobo and Rumpy had needed treatment for skin ailments. She had recommended her own Highland vet when Rumpy had lost Poisti and was left with an udder bursting with milk.

The Littles had suggested Illy milk Rumpy, but Mr. Bacon, Mrs. Paul's vet, had known best.

Mrs. Paul suggested that they phone around to other members of the Highland Society, perhaps someone could offer a field, or at least a place in a herd. The young couple did that, but with each call their hope dwindled. No fields for rent and no place in a herd for a bull without papers. A bull without papers could not be put in with cows and no one had a bull herd to put him into. Sarah had marked off all the names of the Highland Society members who had herds within two hours' driving distance. As the story was always the same – "no space" – she tried one last resort, placing an ad in the *Farmer's Weekly*. It yielded only one offering of a field in their own city. They made an appointment with the owner. Inside they were thrilled and looked forward to returning home with a reason for celebration. The owner had told them the field was near the river. They scanned their map and went to the river an hour before they were due to meet the owner. They looked at the fields stretching along the length of the river and wondered which one might become Bobo's own field.

Happy and confident that Bobo soon might be living near them, they set off to meet the owner outside the nearby restaurant. To their surprise the man told them to follow as he drove away from the river and towards a residential area. He led them down a path through a small wood. Then they turned into an opening which revealed a field, a small field split up into three tiny lots, which were surrounded by houses and blocks of flats. Two of the lots were occupied by horses. The third lot was the one the man was offering for rent.

The young couple could not hide their dejection. How could they put Bobo here? There was so little land that they would be feeding Bobo hay for most of the year. In this residential area he would be exposed to so many people. Would they taunt him and pull his horns? Would he break out and be hit by a car? This was the city, it was not farmland.

Still, they did not turn the man down. They couldn't because this might be Bobo's only chance of survival. They requested time to consider this field while looking for others. The man went along with that. He obviously did not have any other takers for the property. At home Sarah and Illy considered all the possible disadvantages of the field and the advantages. There was only one advantage – Bobo's life would be saved. That was the uppermost advantage and they decided that should they have no more replies to their ads within the week they would seize this opportunity. He wouldn't have to stay there forever. That field would buy them time to continue the search for something better.

In their heart of hearts they did not want that urban field, but a place that could assure Bobo a safe and pastoral life worth living. What sort of life he would have in that field seemed very questionable. The week went by but no further offers came. The couple suffered niggling doubt and dejection. Sarah phoned the man and said they had a few more fields to look at and asked if they could have one more week before giving a definitive answer. The man agreed. No doubt he knew she was lying, but he had no other takers, so what was it to him. A sigh of relief and an extra week's grace gave the young couple renewed hope. What they were hoping for, when the black and white of their situation was so clear, was a miracle, no less. Yes, they were dreamers and believed in miracles.

EIGHT

A MIRACLE
INDEED

Belief moves mountains they say. Well, the belief of Sarah and Illy moved the heart of a member of the Scottish Highland Cattle Society. His name was Dr. Smith. He was an eye doctor who had several herds of Scottish Highlanders. He saw the young couple's ad in the *Farmers' Weekly* and he was moved by how desperately this couple were looking for a field. There was no word of desperation in their ad, but from the size of the field they were looking for, he could tell they were out to save their bull. He phoned to say he had seen their ad and he had seen from the members' list that they, too, belonged to the society. He had no field to offer them as such, but he was keen to get to know other members of the society and he invited them to meet him and visit his herds. He had promised nothing and yet that call filled the young couple with renewed hope. If he couldn't help them, perhaps he knew someone who could.

Summer was in full swing and with the long bright evening ahead the young couple drove off to meet Dr. Smith. They met at seven in the evening. He was a young man and a man who loved his herds. That became very apparent, when they visited the first herd close to the meeting place.

As they watched the herd grazing in the huge pastures, they knew the field in the city would have to be turned down. This is where Bobo belonged. To keep him on his own would be a sin. He was a herd animal. Of course they had not planned to leave Rumpy behind. They had wanted to find Bobo a place and then take Rumpy, but now they saw what Rumpy and Bobo had missed out on all this time. They saw what Rumpy had known and been dragged from. Dr. Smith took the young couple to three other fields that evening. He had a similar relationship to his animals as they had to their friends. Like them, he gave them names, not all of them, as there were so many, but a lot of them. When he called them they came. He would go into the field and spoil them with treats and cuddles. Just like Mrs. Paul, he was an animal's best friend.

The young couple were delighted by the antics of the calves dashing and tumbling together. How different this world was to the one Bobo had known as a calf. In one field there was a cow who had borne twins. She had only accepted one calf to suckle. The people who had rented the field to Dr. Smith lived next to the field, so they bottle-fed the other twin, and he didn't seem to mind this extra attention at all. When the bull calf was called in for his feed and the young couple went in to watch, he walked over to them, gave them a sniff, then a lick and tried to follow them out when they were leaving.

In time Dr. Smith took the couple to a vacant plot of land. It wasn't really a field, such as they imagined, but it was out of the city, quiet, close to farms for hay, so when Dr. Smith said that the young couple could certainly take that, if they wanted, they jumped at the chance. Of course it was much further away from home, but they felt they could manage.

That evening they had visited paradise. They had seen what direction they must take. They knew this place would be the beginning of a future for Bobo, Rumpy and her calf to come. Dr. Smith intimated that it would take a while to get everything arranged. The very next day the young couple phoned the Littles with the good news. They would be taking Bobo. They had a field, and they would be in touch as soon as details had been finalised. That summer was glorious. Bobo was going to live, to live in a new home, and Rumpy would be joining him. Their new calf would be joining them. The young couple turned down the field in the city and celebrated.

Then they began to think about details. They had no trailer. Even if they hired one, their car was not powerful enough to pull it. Perhaps Mrs. Paul might be able to help. They took out the list of society members to find her number when Sarah thought to call Dr. Smith. Of course! A miracle indeed! The next day they received a return call from Dr. Smith. He offered to use his jeep and trailer to transport Bobo, no problem. He had plans to keep young bulls in one field. Bobo could take charge of them. That would be much better, Dr. Smith said, than having him in a small field on his own. The fact that Bobo had no papers would not be a problem so long as he was kept away from cows. The doctor would need the summer to get everything organised. He promised to be in touch.

The young couple were over the moon. Had Dr. Smith perhaps wanted to test their sincerity, before making this offer, or had he made this offer after witnessing how committed these two were to keeping their bull alive? "Their bull"! Bobo wasn't theirs yet, but they instructed the Littles to draw up a contract. They had almost forgotten to consider whether they would be able to afford Bobo's purchase price, transport and upkeep. They would find a way, and a way to save Rumpy from being left on her own to fend off the horses.

The summer passed and Crystal was not happy that Bobo's removal was taking so long. The couple did not feel they could badger the doctor who had banished their worst nightmares. He would be in touch. They would have to wait. It was nearing October and Crystal made it very clear that if Bobo was not removed within a matter of weeks, he would be sent to the slaughterhouse. Illy phoned Dr. Smith. Everything was arranged for October 3rd. The young couple could not sleep the night before Bobo's transport. They worried about what might go wrong. Not only would they have to lure him into the trailer, they would have to stop off at a vet's on the way, so Bobo could get the necessary vaccinations.

In the midst of all these worries was the thought of Rumpy being deprived of her friend and mate yet again. Of course they had planned to take her, but Rumpy didn't know that. Again she would have to suffer. The young couple had already told Dr. Smith of their plans for Rumpy. Dr. Smith had assured them that he could place Rumpy in one of his herds with the understanding that they would have to pay for her upkeep. The couple were not sure if they could financially cover the costs of buying both Rumpy and Bobo and paying for their upkeep, but that was their plan. Rumpy wouldn't have to suffer for long. She would not be able to join Bobo, but she would go into a big herd, back to the life she had known as a calf with Dumpy.

Bobo at three days old.

Bobo at three days old.

Bobo and Sadie.

Bobo and Sadie.

Sadie and Ginger.

Above: Rumpy and Ginger.

Below: Ginger.

Bobo aged 14.

Bobo.

NINE

RITE OF
PASSAGE

At three o'clock in the afternoon of October 3rd Sarah and Illy were at the field waiting for Dr. Smith's trailer. They had filled the boot of their car with goodies to lure Bobo with. The jeep and trailer arrived. Two young men, employees of Dr. Smith, parked the jeep and trailer in the field close to the main gate. They prepared the trailer for loading and then stood back for Illy and Sarah to do their work.

Illy was in the trailer luring Bobo in with food. At first Rumpy started up the ramp, vying for the treats, but mistrusting the strange vehicle, she eventually backed away. Bobo trusted trailers as much, or as little as his mother did, so he ate the food, but barely budged forward. As the abundance of food dwindled, so did the young couple's hope of getting Bobo into the trailer.

An hour had passed and he was still on the ramp. The couple's rations of goodies were so depleted they thought that they would have to concede defeat, when Mr. Scratchback cycled by. They had informed him of the departure date and there he was to bid his friend adieu. He rushed over to the cornfield and, returning with an armful of the corn he knew Bobo loved so well, he saved the day. Bobo, tempted by his favourite delight, slowly but surely entered the trailer and stayed put long enough for Illy to exit by the front door and for the two men to close and secure the back door. Sadly there was no time to comfort Rumpy. They had to get to the vet's for Bobo's vaccinations and then to the field which was an hour's drive away.

When the trailer door was opened for Bobo to step out into his new home, he was lying down. Yes, it had been a traumatic experience for him and it was not to end here. Two young bulls, Disco and Lobster, stood at the trailer bellowing for Bobo to show his face, if he dared. The young couple went into the field and coaxed Bobo out of the trailer. They soon had to beat a hasty retreat when Disco and Lobster decided to test the mettle of this intruder by chasing him from one end of the field to the other. The two young bulls taunted Bobo like two ruffians taunting a school boy. The couple had not been prepared for this. Well, they were city folk. They had little idea of the ways of the herd. Bobo bellowed to his friends, his protectors, but there was nothing they could do, only stand and watch and hope. No doubt Bobo had thought he was the only bull in the world up to this point. Disco and Lobster were younger than Bobo, but they ganged together and set Bobo to flight.

The couple ached inside, listening to the bellows of the friend they now could not help. By seven o' clock it was so dark they could barely see anything. Bobo stood alone under a tree at the top of the hill and bellowed. They had to leave but they left their hearts there, hoping somehow things would work out and Bobo would be happy. They had so looked forward to seeing Bobo alive in a new home, but they drove home dejected and unhappy. They had not reckoned with such treatment. Had they done the right thing?

The next three days Sarah and Illy raced off to Bobo's field. And from there they went to Rumpy's field. They held out their hands covered in Bobo's oils for Rumpy to smell so she would know her mate was all right. She understood what the couple were trying to say and her mourning was different this time. Those first three days were not easy for Bobo. He kept away from the two young bulls, but they ganged up to chase him whenever the mood struck them.

On the third day it seemed that Bobo was preparing to make contact with Lobster. Slowly he approached the young bull and held out his nose to sniff at Lobster's nose. Sarah and Illy hoped this might be the beginning of reconciliation and acceptance, but suddenly Lobster lowered his head and started pushing Bobo back down the hill. Disco joined in and the battle for leadership went into full swing. The couple had never seen Bobo fight as he did that day. He had never had to before. Bobo parried and pushed and as he fought off the one then the other stepped in. Bobo was too strong for the two of them individually, so then the two attacked together.

The couple looked on and grieved. What had they brought him to? Weakened by the joint attack, Bobo gave up and ran over to where his friends stood. His tongue was hanging out and was covered in a milk-white film. He looked exhausted. Then it struck the young couple that Bobo may not have had a drink since his arrival. Illy and Sarah got into the field. Illy walked up the hill to the water fountain and began calling Bobo. Sarah threw bread down to distract the two young bulls and then she escorted her worn-out friend up the hill. He plodded next to his protector up the hill to the water fountain. His thirst confirmed that he had had no water all that time. For twenty minutes he drank, while his protectors stood close by to fend off the ruffians, should they attack again. They didn't. Little did the couple know that what they had witnessed was routine behaviour when a new bull comes into the field. Sarah feared that the two might attack Bobo again. She was calmed by Dr. Smith's assurances that the fight was over. The hierarchy in the field was now established.

It was during this conversation that Dr. Smith told the pair of his visit to the Littles. He had been thinking of Rumpy alone with the horses and had decided to offer to buy her himself. He found the life Rumpy was now exposed to was no life at all for a herd animal. The fact that he had said exactly that to Farmer Little was no doubt the reason why Farmer Little declined his offer to buy Rumpy. She was not for sale. Obviously Farmer Little's pride had been hurt. The couple only hoped that the "not for sale" only applied to Dr. Smith and not to them.

Unfortunately their connection to Dr. Smith blocked their bid to buy Rumpy, too. Crystal explained that Farmer Little was very fond of Rumpy. She would be having a calf the following spring and it was their intention to have her artificially inseminated, so she would calve every year. No need for a bull. The couple, happy that Bobo and the young bulls had now settled down together, were now thrown back into the nightmare they had fought so hard to quell, the nightmare they felt they had conquered. Rumpy was to stay on her own with the giants. Dragon would now be free to get his own back, without Bobo to intervene. Just as when Dumpy was taken, she would have a long wait till her calf came to keep her company. She would have to protect that calf from Atropa, Arine, Speedy and now Dragon. The young couple could protect Rumpy when they were in the field, but their daily visits were one hour in a long day. Rumpy's future and the future of her calf looked more than bleak. Another bull calf would keep the whole vicious circle going.

TEN

NEW FRIENDS

Bobo kept very much to himself in his new home. For the first time in his life he was on his own. Disco and Lobster were fellow bulls, but they were not friends and comforters like Rumpy. They stayed together just as they had before Bobo arrived. Rumpy had also been Bobo's mate. It had been his job to protect her. Now he only had to protect himself. Bobo also missed not having a stable here to rest in or to shelter in from the cold. While Disco and Lobster lay side by side at night, Bobo spent the cold nights alone. When the trio took a nap they took up the same positions, Disco and Lobster side by side and Bobo a healthy distance away on his own. That was how Sarah and Illy always sighted them.

They hoped in time that Bobo would be allowed into the inner circle. At least he had a new home and the two ruffians were leaving Bobo to his own devices. In the old field Bobo had used the telephone pole as a scratching post. Here there was a metal pylon with a sturdy cement base, excellent for rubbing and scratching activities. There were also two trees, one at either end of the field. They, too, offered excellent rubbing facilities. From the surrounding farms came the cackle of geese, the bleating of lambs, the neighing of horses and the clucking of hens. The odd fox would use Bobo's field as a shortcut to the farms. The rest of the daily sounds echoing around the field were those of tractors, cars and dogs. The dogs didn't march by as they had at the old field. They kept to the properties they were there to defend. This was the world Bobo now shared with the two young bulls.

Disco and Lobster proved to have really entertaining personalities. Whenever Sarah and Illy arrived and called to Bobo, they, too, would join the couple at the fence. Disco had a swagger in his gait. He was the king, no doubt about that. Lobster, though built like a tank, was a more gentle personality. He seemed to be Disco's minion. Disco was the brains and Lobster was the brawn. Disco did the talking and Lobster did what he was told. The two didn't hang round at the fence for long. Disco would always go off first and Lobby would always follow.

Thus Bobo enjoyed undisturbed feeding and grooming when his friends came to visit. Sadly that was no longer a daily event any more, for Sarah and Illy could not manage visits every day to Rumpy and to Bobo's new field, which was now a two hour drive there and back. Bobo was grateful for these visits, the only link between his past and his present life. Sarah and Illy often mentioned Rumpy's name when talking to Bobo, so the couple trusted that he knew all must be well with her. Though all else had changed, they were still the same old friends.

During their visits to Bobo Sarah and Illy got to know Mr Dicky. He had rented the field to Dr. Smith. He was a wealthy pensioner who lived in a big house next to Bobo's field. He had been a butcher most of his working life, but then he had won the lottery. Now the former butcher enjoyed spoiling the trio with vegetables from his garden and stale bread rolls from his friend, the baker. He was the one who gave the trio their hay and who kept a watchful eye on the water fountain. At the first sign of icy weather he barricaded the water fountain with bales of straw and took on the job of filling the bathtub in the field and breaking any layers of ice that formed. The trio accepted Mr. Dicky as one of the herd. He looked on his three boys as the best behaved choristers, for they bellowed their greetings when he arrived with their food. Whatever jobs Mr. Dicky had to do in the field he was left to do them in peace.

One job, however, did cause consternation to the trio as well as to Sarah and Illy. On that occasion Mr. Dicky was walking across the meadow with a tool in his hand when he was swallowed up by the field, or so it seemed. One minute he was there. The next moment he was gone. Disco walked to where he had last seen Mr. Dicky and just stood looking down at the ground. What Sarah and Illy didn't know was that Disco was standing over the manhole Mr. Dicky had disappeared down into and now wished to get out of. Eventually Disco moved and to the young couple's surprise Mr. Dicky climbed up out into the field again.

Outwardly it seemed that Bobo had come to terms with the trauma of leaving his old home and his mate, Rumpy, and of his stormy welcome into his new home. However, Sarah and Illy knew that Bobo was very sensitive, so when his fur began to full out, they guessed it was a physical reaction to all the pain and loss he had been through. For two months they treated Bobo's hair loss. Dr. Bacon prescribed the treatment. The couple had to spray every inch of Bobo's fur and then brush the substance in. Bobo accepted this ritual. He turned and positioned himself as requested. Lobster and Disco, on the other hand, took one whiff of the foul reeking substance and they were off. The problem was the winter weather. Sarah and Illy had to rush to the field on days the temperature allowed a treatment. Often it was too cold and they had to wait. After two months and endless treatments Bobo's fur began to grow back on the bald patches.

Now after each visit to Bobo's field the couple felt more content. Not only did their bull have a friend in Mr. Dicky, but other locals began to visit and bring him tidbits. Lobster would hang round at the fence with Bobo when the couple were there. Disco would make a brief appearance and then be off on his own. So gradually Bobo and Lobster became friends and playmates. By spring they were "horsing" around just as Bobo and Dragon had done.

ELEVEN

GINGER

As Bobo was gaining a friend in his new world, Rumpy was ready to welcome her newborn. Farmer Little had not forgotten what had happened to Rumpy's last calf, so a few weeks before the anticipated birth, he took the horses down to the tiny field. Sarah and Illy were most pleased about that development. Admittedly the new calf would not alter the old tradition of "there had always been two," but like Farmer Little, they did not want to leave anything to chance either. Atropa had given them reason not to trust her this time.

Eagerly the couple and the other regulars waited for the new addition and they all prayed that it would be a cow-calf this time. The evening before the birth Sarah and Illy were with Rumpy. She was ravenous for cuddles and sweating through her long fur. The couple were sure the calf would arrive that night or early the next morning. They set their alarms for an early rise and immediately drove over to the field. Standing outside the horses' stable they could see where Rumpy had delivered her calf in the sand. They peeked into the stable and there with Rumpy was her little calf, looking fragile and frail, standing in the corner.

Rumpy had not yet given her calf a "tongue bath," for it was still covered in sand and film from the birth. In its present condition it seemed the calf's fur was grey. Sarah and Illy congratulated Rumpy and made a fuss of her. She was ravenous for the titbits they had brought. Giving birth is no easy task. No wonder she was hungry. Illy fetched a portion of pellets for her and put them in her bucket. She wolfed them down. While Rumpy ate, the couple watched her calf and wondered if their prayers had been answered. Illy went over to the calf and picked her up. Rumpy showed no concern. She continued to eat. Illy looked for the tell-tale signs and announced that it was indeed a cow calf. Double celebrations were now called for. Rumpy then lay down in the straw and Sarah and Illy sat down with her. The calf positioned herself behind her mother and lay down, too. The couple were just leaning back enjoying the wonderful atmosphere in the stable, when Rumpy's head fell back and it seemed she was dead.

Though numb with panic Sarah stumbled along the path to the nearby house. She asked the owners to phone Farmer Little, which they did. When Sarah got back to the stable Rumpy was back in her lying position. Illy felt sure that she had briefly passed out because of the strain of the birth. Farmer Little was sure that the titbits and pellets had caused Rumpy's blackout and he ordered Sarah and Illy to leave Rumpy in peace that day. They did as they were told but the following day they were back at the field to greet Rumpy and Ginger, for that was the name they had chosen for the new calf. When they called to Rumpy she appeared from the stable with Ginger in tow. The grey colour had now been thoroughly licked away to reveal a beautiful coat of reddish brown with large patches of white and four white socks. Ginger already looked sturdier and taking his camera Illy took a picture of his three favourite girls, Sarah, Rumpy and Ginger.

The regulars were as overjoyed as the young couple and they got to see a lot more of Ginger than they had of Bobo as a young calf. Rumpy kept close to the stable the first week. The horses were still in the tiny field, so there was no danger, but Rumpy was still cautious. She was no doubt remembering what had happened to Poisti. By the third week both mother and calf were out in the field but always in the top half. Rumpy did not venture down to the bottom with her calf for there she would be in sight of the giants.

Spring was in fall swing and the horses were still in the tiny field. Rumpy and Ginger were happy and content, so were Sarah, Illy and the regulars. As had been the case with Bobo, Ginger became the star attraction of the field. Visitors marvelled at her unusual markings. Illy researched the question of colour and markings and found out that there were basically eight different types: red, black, blonde, dun, white, grey, brindled, and red with white markings. Ginger belonged to the last type, which had become quite rare. Farmer Little was equally aware of what a prize specimen Rumpy had given birth to. Yes, Ginger was something special. It took her a while to understand her mother's relationship with the young couple, but gradually she came to trust them.

Sarah and Illy visited Rumpy and Ginger every day. When Rumpy had had her treats and brushing, she would stride off munching away at the luscious green grass.

Once Ginger had come to accept and seek the joy of being brushed and rubbed, she stayed with Sarah and Illy enjoying the abundance of attention she got. She would play with them – running off, then circling to run back, kicking the air where they stood, but to run off again. When she tired of games, she would drop down at Sarah's feet to rest. They would sit together, with Ginger resting her head on Sarah's lap or legs. Their relationship had begun when Ginger was only a few weeks old. One day very slowly and hesitantly Ginger had first made her way over to Sarah. Sensing the calf's approach, Sarah kept her position, not budging an inch, for fear of frightening the little one. She suddenly felt Ginger's nose first sniffing at her cheek, then her hair and her cap. Ginger then gave her cheek a gentle lick. As Sarah tried to turn, Ginger jumped back in the direction of her mother and never came close again for weeks.

Now Ginger was three months old and she treated Sarah and Illy like "aunts." Rumpy and Ginger were so happy in "their" paradise, Sarah and Illy wondered how long that paradise would continue. Ginger knew nothing of the giants, but she would get to know them. Of that the couple were sure. The whole summer long the horses remained in the tiny field and in the big field joy was had by one and all.

TWELVE

LEAD BULL

Just as much joy was being had in Bobo's new field. Disco had been taken off to a new herd at the beginning of the summer and the two pals, Lobster and Bobo, had been given recruits to look after. Three young bulls, Red, Didi and Grey joined Bobo's Academy of Bull Education. For the first time in his life, Bobo was the lead bull and Lobster, as had always been the case in his life, gladly took the post of second-in-command. Bobo took to his new role as a babe to its mother's milk, "mother" being the operative word, for indeed he mothered the new recruits. He tolerated no straying from the herd, and when it came to nap time he would stand over his boys and Lobster, ready to protect them from any danger. He took his job so seriously he fairly wore himself out, but clearly he loved his charges and the duty of caring for them.

When it came to playtime, Bobo gave his recruits lessons in combat. They marvelled at how he could take all three of them on with "one horn tied behind his back." He was an expert – that was obvious. The recruits sought Lobster out for their mounting games. Lobster had never enjoyed these games as a youngster. When Disco had begun such tactics, Lobster had taken to his heels. When he himself tried, he showed that he had had little schooling in such matters, for when he tried to mount Disco, which was not very often, he always mounted from the front, holding onto Disco's horns with his front legs, apparently thinking they were handles. In his new role, Lobster tolerated the young recruits' mounting tactics, up to a point that is, for as long as they were members of Bobo's Academy.

Sarah and Illy were delighted with the camaraderie in Bobo's field. The new boys were entertaining and Bobo was content in his role. He still came for his treats and cuddles, but when duty called, he'd be off to tend to his boys, only returning to the couple once he was assured all was well. Lobster spent as much time at the fence with Sarah and Illy as Bobo did, for he too loved the human touch. As for the treats they brought, Bobo allowed Lobster and his boys their share – that was only fair. Grey was the most aloof of the young Highlanders, a prince among paupers. He came from noble stock and seemed to know it. He had a beautiful grey velvet coat, magnificent proportions and a regal gait. In time young Grey was intended to be sold to a farm in Sweden for a handsome price.

Red and Didi were more playful characters. Didi looked a lot like the young Disco, whereas Red had more of young

Disco's confidence. Yet it was Red who was the first to require Bobo's help. The boys and Lobster had settled down for a nap, while Bobo was being groomed by Illy and Sarah. Red obviously wanted to get up again but he couldn't, for he had made a grave mistake. He had positioned himself on the slope with his legs uphill and his head and shoulders downhill. Bobo immediately reacted to Red's panic. He walked over to his young recruit and bending down he pressed against Red's head and shoulders with his horns. He then lifted the distressed bull's head, looked, and repeated the procedure. This went on for quite a while, but eventually Bobo got Red into the necessary position for him to stand up. Having saved the day, Bobo returned to his friends and Red decided to keep on his legs and went off to nibble grass.

By the end of the summer there were changes in both Rumpy's and Bobo's fields. Bobo and his boys were moved to a field fifty yards down from their present location, which now offered only meagre stubble. As the distance was minimal Dr. Smith decided that he and his men would herd Bobo and the adolescents along the narrow road down to their new field. The gate was opened and Bobo, as lead bull, took front position and led the way. Reaching the open gate of the new field Bobo suddenly stopped, signalled his charges to wait as he proceeded to check out their new home, scouting its perimeters and sniffing at the ground. Satisfied all was in order, Bobo gave the boys a signal and in they marched.

When Sarah and Illy heard about the move they regretted not having been there to see Bobo's grand show of command. The new field was much bigger than the old one and it had lots of grass. Near the main gate there was a feeder and two rows of giant hay bales prepared for winter feeding. At the far end of the field there was a stream, so there would be no need for Mr. Dicky to provide the boys' water supply. Bobo and the boys were happy in their new field. Sarah and Illy were happy too.

THIRTEEN

ON THE HORNS
OF A DILEMMA

They were not at all happy with the changes that occurred in Rumpy's field, although they had reckoned with them for a long time. The horses had returned to the big field which meant the biting and chasing games resumed. Sarah and Illy were most unhappy when they saw the bite marks on Rumpy's side. Their first thought was "Dragon's getting his own back, now." Farmer Little was well aware of what had been happening, so he put up an electric fence to form an enclosure for Rumpy and Ginger. Their paddock was small but the electric fence kept the horses away, so at least there was no more biting, though peace and quiet was not assured, as Dragon loved to intimidate the two whenever he passed by on his way out to the field. Ginger was absolutely petrified at the sight of him. Rumpy pretended to ignore the upstart. Dragon got very cheeky with Illy and Sarah on occasions, but Illy put him in his place and he often showed immediate regret for what he had done to them. There was no regret for his intimidation of Rumpy and Ginger.

Illy and Sarah wondered how the bulls would fare in the coming winter. Conflict with the horses created a stressful life for Rumpy and Ginger. Obviously the couple were not the only ones who considered the situation somewhat impossible. A few weeks later Illy received a phone call from Farmer Little offering Rumpy and Ginger for sale. If the couple could not buy them, then they would be sold off to someone else. They had to go one way or the other, and as soon as possible. Buying them was one thing, but the couple would need a field for them. Illy phoned Dr. Smith who immediately suggested that the couple buy Rumpy and Ginger and sell them on to him. Then he would put them into one of his herds.

The couple stressed that at some point in the future they hoped to own Bobo, Rumpy, and Ginger themselves. The doctor promised to stipulate in the contract of sale that should he himself ever wish to sell Rumpy and Ginger, he would have to offer them to the young couple first. As Farmer Little had stressed that the move should take place as soon as possible, the doctor promised to have the two moved within a week. Two days later the sales contract arrived. Sarah and Illy signed immediately and transferred the agreed sum to Farmer Little's account.

Dr. Smith had arranged for one of his men to bring the trailer to the field and to help with the loading. Sarah and Illy arranged with Farmer Little for the horses to be taken down to the tiny field so they would cause no disturbance on the day of the move.

The old regulars were sad to think they wouldn't be seeing Rumpy and Ginger again, but their sadness was mixed with joy at the thought of the girls going to a herd and leading a normal life at last. As had been the case before Bobo had been moved, Sarah and Illy worried about getting the two into the trailer. Rumpy hated trailers. They felt Ginger was more likely to lead the way.

On the day of the move the skies opened up and the rain poured down. Sarah and Illy filled the car with treats to lure their friends into the trailer. They drove to the field and waited. None of the regulars were there to see the girls off, as the rain was just coming down in buckets. The trailer arrived and despite their initial nervousness both Rumpy and Ginger followed Illy to the trailer and began to eat the treats Illy had scattered along the ramp to tempt them in.

Rumpy seemed particularly ravenous, so much so that she wouldn't let Ginger get onto the ramp to share the treats. Slowly Rumpy followed the trail of titbits into the trailer. Cautiously the young man got out of the jeep and in a flash Rumpy was trapped. The helper struggled to get the metal dividing frame in place to block the cow's way out. Panic forced every drop of urine and dung out of Rumpy's body. She tried to turn, but to no avail. It had taken half an hour to get her in, but now she was in and the worst was over, or so Sarah and Illy thought. They went into the trailer to comfort Rumpy.

They then called to Ginger but she looked at them and ran. They had not reckoned with that. They left the trailer and walked over to her. She was nervous and despite allowing them to stroke her, she would not follow them to the trailer.

The young man, by now a little impatient, suggested they herd Ginger into the trailer. Sarah and Illy were not too happy about the idea and didn't think it would work, but they did not know what else they could do. They were all soaking wet and hoping for a quick solution. That quick solution didn't come. Ginger dodged their attempts and the more they tried the more she panicked. The young man produced a rope. All three held the rope to form a type of fence, and began herding again, to no avail. Ginger was beside herself. What were her friends and that man doing to her? What had she and her mother done to deserve this?

The young man suggested that they tie the rope around Ginger's horns and pull her. There was nothing else they could do but attempt it. Sarah and Illy did not wish to try it. Her horns were short, only just growing. They might break. But what else could they do. Rumpy had been locked in the trailer over an hour already. Dr. Smith had arranged everything for that day. They couldn't give up.

The assistant walked away and Sarah and Illy walked over to Ginger. She no longer trusted them as she had before, but she was so in need of reassurance that she slowly but hesitantly allowed them to stroke her. They comforted her for quite a while. They began to walk over to where the rope lay on the ground and she took a few steps and stopped. They went back and cuddled and comforted her again. They repeated this procedure, eventually coaxing her over to where the rope lay. Sarah cuddled Ginger, while Illy got the rope ready. They knew they would only get one stab at this. Illy succeeded in getting the rope over both horns and he and Sarah held on tight. The young man appeared and he and

Illy began pulling. As small as Ginger was – she was only six months old – she was like the immoveable object. She barely budged, so the more the two men pulled the more her horns had to take the pressure. Sarah panicked when she saw one horn bending as if it were going to break in two.

"Leave her, leave her," she screamed, "her horn is breaking." The two men let go of the rope and Ginger bolted. Two hours they had tried to get Ginger into the trailer. For two hours Rumpy had been barricaded in the trailer. To think that Sarah and Illy had reckoned with trouble from Rumpy but not from Ginger. There was no more they could do. Rumpy was let out of the trailer and the young man drove off. Three hours in the pouring rain and the couple were back to square one – no, not even square one, for now Ginger no longer trusted them. Rumpy came down the ramp and immediately headed for Sarah and Illy. They expected to get a chop from her horn, but they didn't. She begged for stroking and reassurance. The couple cuddled her gladly and felt like crying. After all they had put her through, she wanted their affection. They tried to comfort Ginger but she now kept her distance. They stayed at the field for another twenty minutes and then returned home to get into some dry clothes and to call Farmer Little and Dr. Smith.

The couple called Dr. Smith first. He was sorry to hear that the move hadn't worked out and suggested that he come personally the following week and dart the cow and her calf with an anaesthetic, so as to make the move easier. Illy called Farmer Little to pass on the news. For the next few days Ginger would not let Illy and Sarah near her. Rumpy was as friendly as ever, but that did not seem to influence Ginger's feelings, and rightly so, the couple thought. In Ginger's eyes what they had done was unforgiveable. They had totally abused her trust.

Three days before the next attempt Ginger began to be her old self again with the couple. Sarah and Illy were happy but worried about how Ginger would react after being darted. Whatever, they enjoyed Ginger's renewed trust and they enjoyed being with Ginger and Rumpy in the big field, no electric fences any more, no horses, who were being kept down in the tiny field until Rumpy and Ginger were moved.

The day before the move Sarah and Illy arrived at the field to find Ginger standing like an immoveable statue. They called but she did not move. Sarah got in and walked over to her. The poor thing had a cord around her neck. Sarah immediately recognised what the cord was. It was from a bale of hay. But how had she got it over her head? She removed it and cuddled her friend. She produced the treat bag, but Ginger would not eat anything. She was not her usual self. Had someone tried to take her from the field? Was it she did not want to eat or she could not eat, for the cord had been pulled so tightly round her neck? Rumpy was her usual self, so was it just an accident? Sarah was happy that the two would be away into a herd the very next day. The next day could not come soon enough.

FOURTEEN
REUNION

When Dr. Smith arrived at the field Sarah and Illy were there waiting. He had left the Land Rover and the trailer parked at the bottom of the narrow road so as not to upset the animals. He had his dart gun in a case, so there was nothing visibly threatening. He told Sarah and Illy what he was going to do and what he wanted them to do. Sarah and Illy went into the field and began feeding Rumpy and Ginger. While the girls were distracted, Dr. Smith removed his gun from its case and inserted a dart. He called to the couple to move to one side, and in a flash a large fat dart was hanging from Rumpy's flank. She immediately bolted and kicked at the air, trying to shake it off. Rumpy had to calm down and stop running or she would have a heart attack, the doctor warned. Sarah rushed over to Rumpy and began comforting her. Ginger was panicking too, and ran over to Illy. Dr Smith got into the field and darted Ginger. Illy broke out in a sweat realising how close the dart had come to penetrating his own flank. Thankfully, Dr. Smith was an excellent marksman.

Within a very short time Rumpy and Ginger sank to the ground, and were knocked out. Sarah and Illy knelt next to their friends and stroked them. Dr Smith got his men to drive the trailer into the field and then everyone waited for the girls to come round. Passers-by enquired whether the two were dead. Indeed that's how they looked lying on the ground. Dr. Smith said it could take an hour to two hours for them to awaken. Patience was the name of the game. It was indeed an hour and a half before the girls began trying to get back on their feet. As soon as the drowsy animals were walking, Dr. Smith's men slowly pushed Rumpy then Ginger up the ramp into the trailer. Sarah and Illy got into their car, ready to follow the trailer to their girls' new home. As they drove down the narrow road past the horses in the tiny field, they said good-bye to all that had been and looked forward to all that was to come. Little did they know that the trailer was heading for Mr. Dicky's field, Bobo's first field after his move. Bobo would be seeing his Rumpy again and the daughter he had never known.

As Rumpy and Ginger stumbled out of the trailer still very groggy from the darts, Sarah and Illy breathed a sigh of relief. Dr. Smith informed them that he would keep the girls there for a few months before they would join a herd. He and his men drove off and Sarah and Illy got into the field with treats and cuddles in abundance. Though groggy, they were hungry for both. No loss of trust this time, both girls sought reassurance and got it. Now Sarah and Illy had their three friends together. They wondered how Bobo would react to having Rumpy nearby. Hopefully he would not break out.

They drove back there the very next day to find the girls back to normal standing down at the bottom looking over at Bobo's field. Bobo was at the gate to his field looking over at his friend and mate Rumpy. Bellows were exchanged, but Bobo stayed put in his own field guarding his boys. They too showed interest in the two arrivals across the fence, but Bobo kept them in check. They did not attempt to break through to the girls' field. For the next four weeks the bulls and cows went about their separate business, with a few daily breaks for exchanging bellows at the fence. Then Sarah and Illy arrived at the field to find Lobster had been put in with Rumpy and Ginger.

FIFTEEN

BOBO
DETHRONED

Bobo was by no means amused, but Lobster seemed over the moon with this new development. The reason soon became clear. Lobster was a breeding bull. Rumpy, it turned out, was not expecting a calf at all, so Lobster's visit might mean a summer calf for Rumpy. Lobster enjoyed the ladies' company for the following four weeks. Then he was returned to Bobo's field and Bobo's rage. Bobo would not associate with his old pal. He just ignored him. Lobster spent most of his time at the gate bellowing over to "his" ladies. He was little bothered by the loss of Bobo's friendship, for his eyes belonged to Rumpy.

Unfortunately Lobster did not have long to ogle at his ladies from across the fence, for a week later, just before Christmas, Rumpy and Ginger were moved to a herd of cows. So great were Lobster's feelings for his ladies that he broke out the day they were moved and went in search of his girls. He looked a sorrowful sight making his way up the road, passing through the open gate and wandering about the field, which now only held the memories of his days of glory among the harem. Breaking out from Bobo's herd to seek out Bobo's mate only widened the gap between these former pals. Sarah and Illy hoped that time would heal Bobo's wounds and the two would become friends again.

Their hope was broken by another profound event that changed the dynamics among the bulls. In January a massive bull was put into Bobo's field. When Sarah and Illy saw him they couldn't believe their eyes. He looked so much like Disco, but could Disco have grown so much since his departure? It was indeed Disco, a giant Disco. It was obvious to Sarah and Illy the fight for leadership had taken place, and the winner was not Bobo but Disco. Bobo was no longer in command. Didi and Grey kept by his side avowing their support, but Bobo's expression was one of loss and misery. Red showed a playful interest in Disco and Lobster kept to himself and his memories of Rumpy. This traumatic experience in Bobo's life expressed itself in weight loss, hair loss and loss of the old spirit. Disco went his own way, he didn't mother the youngsters as Bobo had done. The youngsters hung around Bobo as they had before, but their attention couldn't lift Bobo's spirit.

Lobster also rallied around his old pal, but Bobo was too concerned with his misery. He no longer ignored Lobster, but he was unable to pull himself together. Sarah and Illy were aware of what was happening and they talked to Dr. Smith, who assured them that Bobo would get over his loss in time. However, when the doctor saw Bobo some weeks later, he too was so concerned for his health that he advised Sarah and Illy to send a stool sample to the lab, as he feared that Bobo might have contracted some illness. They did as the doctor ordered, and though pleased to receive the report saying there was no sign of serious illness, they wondered how they could stop their friend from wasting away.

By spring Bobo was but a shadow of himself. Admittedly they had just come through a hard winter, but he had shown no loss of appetite during that winter. When Sarah and Illy had been there he had always tucked into the massive bale of hay in the feeder. The answer to their prayers came when Disco was moved off to another herd. Didi and Red were sold and three young bulls, Stan, Olly and Blacky came to take their place. Bobo regained his leadership and again had very young bulls to mother. Lobster was restored to second-in-command and being a pal, while Grey was still an old, trustworthy supporter. These developments brought new life into Bobo, who began to fatten up and become playful once again. Sarah and Illy had always known that Bobo was a particularly sensitive bull. Now that they had their belief confirmed, they hoped that his present reign would last for as long as possible.

SIXTEEN
NEW PASTURES

Rumpy and Ginger were also exposed to the necessary shoving and pushing that establishes hierarchy among cows. There were six older cows in the herd they joined, all much bigger than Rumpy. She pushed and shoved valiantly yet remained in the lowest position among the older cows, though she did have the status and authority to rule the younger cows. After Rumpy and Ginger had been in the herd a few weeks, they seemed a lot more settled. They too had a feeder in the field, but their position in the heirarchy required them to wait for their hay until the older cows had had their fill. They had never had to queue up for their food before, but they got used to this arrangement.

Ginger stuck very close to her mother, and Rumpy was always at the ready to protect her daughter when needed. They had been in the herd just over a month when Fred, a young white bull was put in with them. The poor fellow bellowed for days. Surrounded by so many ladies he bellowed for the one lady he wished to have by his side, his mother. Eventually he stopped bellowing and resigned himself to a loner's existence. He was always off on his own, far away from the others and he, too, being at the bottom of the pole, had a long wait until he could stand undisturbed at the feeder.

When Illy and Sarah visited Rumpy and Ginger, they would get into the field and position themselves at the feeder so that their friends could get in some early mouthfuls of hay. The older cows were not overjoyed about such tactics, but, as they were sufficiently bothered by the presence of these two humans in their field, they moved away in order to keep distance between themselves and the strangers. Fred was wary of the strangers too, but being low on the hierarchy himself, his desire for hay overcame his fear of the strangers and he would join Rumpy and Ginger at the feeder. Though Rumpy would try to chase the upstart away, Ginger seemed less bothered about Fred's proximity, so with time the two became friendlier toward each other.

Any chance of cementing their friendship was dashed when Dr. Smith's trailer arrived one Saturday to remove Rumpy and Ginger from the herd. By chance Sarah and Illy were in the field grooming their friends when Dr. Smith and his men arrived. They had never witnessed the procedure of singling animals out for transport but they immediately saw that the herd knew what was coming and instinctively they all raced towards the top field, the one furthest away from the trailer now parked in the field near the gate. In her panic Ginger raced off in the opposite direction. Reaching the perimeter fence she turned to find she was totally isolated from the herd. The only being in sight was Sarah, who was still standing where Ginger had left her as she had raced off. In her panic she raced at full speed towards Sarah. Illy was down at the gate talking to Dr. Smith. Sarah was numb with fear. Ginger was racing full speed towards her. Sarah knew she had to stand absolutely still. She knew Ginger would not career into her, but fear hammered at this belief and her wish to run away made her shake. As Ginger got closer, there was no reduction in her speed. Sarah held out her arm pointing to Rumpy and the others in the top field and began shouting, "Rumpy's over there. Over there!" Ginger continued coming at full speed and Sarah continued shouting. Ginger was but ten yards from Sarah when she swerved in the direction Sarah had been pointing to. Ginger raced up the field to her mother and Sarah, breathing a sigh of relief, began walking down to the gate to Illy and Dr. Smith.

Dr. Smith's men were hard at work erecting the metal corral they had brought with them in the trailer. Once the corral was ready, three young men walked into the top field to start herding the now panic-stricken clan. As the young men fanned out, the herd raced into the adjoining field. To Sarah it seemed like watching a buffalo stampede. Some of the older cows had calved only the month before and Sarah was amazed how those young calves kept up with the herd. Their way back blocked, the herd had to run on into the bottom field where the corral was waiting for them. Once in the corral the corral gate was secured and the herd began pushing and shoving in an attempt to get out. Sarah was sure that the young calves would be trampled to death, but of course they weren't. Though the herd was very much aware of where the little ones moved, the bellowing of the cows and the cries of the baby calves disturbed Sarah.

Three men got into the corral with the herd. Again Sarah was sure that one of them would be trampled, but it was obvious that despite the commotion, the herd had no wish to hurt the men or themselves. The cattle pushed to get away from the men, away from the "tunnel" that led to the trailer and back to the field.

The men inside the corral began pushing forward to force the herd toward the tunnel and into the trailer. As soon as a cow sensed that she was being shunted into the tunnel, she began to push back and turn away. The attempted flight of the cows seemed to go on for ages. Then one cow unable to fight her way back was flushed into the tunnel. It was Ginger. Illy and Sarah spoke words of comfort and she slowly moved along the tunnel to the section that led out into the trailer. The gate at the end of the tunnel was a device that could be opened and closed quickly, trapping the cow's head in a clamp so that she could not wield her horns. Held firmly in place, ear tags could be affixed, blood samples taken, or necessary injections given. Ginger was given her ear tags and then released onto the ramp of the trailer. Rumpy watched her daughter and friend disappearing into the trailer and voluntarily went into the tunnel to receive her ear tags. She then walked up the ramp into the trailer to join her friend.Sarah and Illy went to their car and followed the trailer to Rumpy's and Ginger's new home. They were to spend the summer with a breeding bull and his herd. Little did Sarah and Illy know that they were accompanying their friends to Disco's summer residence.

Disco's herd consisted of three big blonde cows and their calves and a Frisian cow and her bull calf. Though Rumpy and Ginger were again at the bottom of the hierarchy, this didn't affect their feeding habits, as their new fields were carpeted with luscious grass. On their visits to this herd Sarah and Illy got to see more of Disco, who eventually welcomed their treats and affection. He did not overindulge as was the case with Lobster. He would enjoy a few tidbits and cuddles, then would stroll off to leave Illy and Sarah with their friends. Rumpy was obviously going to have Lobster's calf in the summer. No doubt Disco would sire a calf the following year. Hopefully he would not show interest in Ginger as she was only fifteen months old.

As it happened Disco never had the opportunity to court Ginger. Only four weeks after her move to Disco's herd, Ginger was moved to a herd of black Highland cows. For the first time in her life she would be on her own having to cope alone in a herd of strangers. Sarah and Illy walked with her in her new field. She led, and like her herd, they followed. Then Ginger walked off into her new life. The couple were pacing the top field when they first caught sight of her head just visible among a sea of black cows. Once the sniffing, butting and parrying was over, Ginger settled in to eating, so the couple left and drove back to assure Rumpy that all was well with Ginger in the same way they had reassured her about Bobo's well-being when he had been taken from her.

Bobo and his boys also underwent another move, but to a familiar territory. They were marched back to Mr. Dicky's field along the narrow familiar road. Now the grass was green and luscious and the sun kept them company till evening.

The long journey was only just beginning for Sarah and Illy and their Highland friends. The adventure would continue for many years to come, bringing unexpected joys, sorrows and joys again at every bend in the road. Yet there, in those lush pastures of summer so long ago, they knew they had arrived.

ABOUT THE AUTHOR

Sadie Murphy was born in Birmingham's Irish community in 1948. She went to Bangor University, where she studied German and French. Soon after finishing her studies, she moved to Germany and taught English, Drama and Art at a *Gymnasium* (grammar school) for many years, where her poetry and theatre groups received a great deal of acclaim in the media and won the German President's History Prize for a play they wrote and performed about the Holocaust. During her time in Germany, she and her husband spent nearly twenty years looking after the Scottish Highland Cattle they rescued from slaughter.

In 2008 they moved on to Estonia, where she taught at university for a year before retiring.

She moved back to Birmingham with her husband in 2014 and died of coronavirus in 2020.

Her poetry has appeared over the years in various literary magazines and anthologies in Ireland and Germany. *Wandering Towards Dawn* (Lapwing) is a volume of her own poetry and her husband Ilmar Lehtpere's. Her work has been translated into Irish, Macedonian and Romanian. She co-translated *Presence* and *Currant Beads* (Allikaäärne) by the Estonian poet Mathura. The first edition of *Highland Journey* was published in a limited edition in the US by New Feral Press in 2013.

ACKNOWLEDGEMENT

Many thanks to Joan Digby and New Feral Press for producing the lovely first edition of this book in 2013.